B 945. M2984 M22

HERBERT MARCUSE

MODERN MASTERS

EDITED BY frank kermode

herbert marcuse

AN EXPOSITION AND A POLEMIC

alasdair macintyre

NEW YORK | THE VIKING PRESS

CONTENTS

BIOGRAPHICAL NOTE

Herbert Marcuse was born in Berlin in 1898. He was a student at the University of Berlin and the University of Freiburg, where he studied with Heidegger and from which he received his Ph.D. for a dissertation on Hegel's ontology and its relation to his philosophy of history. On the coming to power of the Nazis he left Germany for Switzerland and taught at Geneva for a year. He then went to the United States, and from 1934 to 1940 was the colleague of Max Horkheimer at the Institute for Social Research, which had emigrated from Frankfurt to Columbia University. He returned to Columbia ten years later, after serving with the Office of Intelligence Research in the State Department, where he was finally Acting Head of the Eastern European section. At Columbia's Russian Institute and Harvard's Russian Research Center he pursued the research which led to the writing of *Soviet Marxism*. From 1954 to 1967 he was at Brandeis University and spent periods as a director of studies at the École Pratique des Hautes Études in Paris. Since 1967 he has taught at the University of California.

HERBERT MARCUSE

Marcuse's Early Doctrine

i

One key task of philosophy is to criticize other philosophy, not only—even if most importantly— in the interests of truth but also because, whether philosophers will it so or not, philosophical ideas are influential in social, moral, and political life. It is part of the quality of life in the present age that those philosophers whose concern for rigor and truth has been most marked have also for the most part been those philosophers who have exhibited least concern about the character of that influence. Whereas those philosophers who have been anxious that what they say should be socially relevant have for the most part been careless and unrigorous and therefore unreliable guides to truth.

Herbert Marcuse has by some of his disciples been elevated to the status of a prophet; he did not choose that status and it would be grossly unfair to judge his thought in terms of it. But he did choose to sustain the role of a persistent critic of modern thought and of its relation to modern society. As such a critic, he has been an influential guide to the political left. It ought therefore to be of great concern to anyone committed to a radical critique of the existing social order to ask simply: Is what Marcuse says true? It will be my crucial contention in this book that almost all of Marcuse's key positions are false. But precisely because this is what I am going to maintain, I am under an exceptional obligation to portray what Marcuse says faithfully. I have therefore tried to separate out sections of exposition from sections of criticism. In distinguishing Marcuse's thought chronologically I have followed Marcuse himself; excepting only for his early doctoral work on Hegel and his contemporaneous writing on Marx, which I have not noticed separately from his later expositions. Marcuse as a young academic was very much a product of the German academic and philosophical tradition, admiring and learning from, for example, Heidegger at Freiburg. How could it have been otherwise? But Marcuse acquired his own specific doctrine precisely as and because he turned away from and against that tradition of thought. He turned against it partly for purely philosophical reasons and partly because he thought he had discovered the sinister character of its relationship to social reality.

Marcuse received his doctorate in philosophy just as the Nazis came to power. He already seems to have accepted that Marxist view of that rise to power according to which Nazism was the political expression of the class interests of the bourgeoisie. By this Marcuse did not merely mean—what is certainly true—that the industrially and financially powerful in Germany had allied themselves with Hitler and had done so in order that he might enable them to dominate the working class by eliminating the Communist and Social Democratic parties and destroying the trade unions. Marcuse held also to a stronger thesis, that Nazism represented a culminating stage in the development of a bourgeois society based on a capitalist economy, such that in the philosophy and theory of Nazism one found the culmination of tendencies present throughout the bourgeois epoch. The characteristic doctrine of earlier bourgeois society was liberalism; but now in the nineteen-thirties the same social structure that had generated liberal thought had generated totalitarian thought. One ought not, therefore, to treat liberalism and totalitarianism as fundamentally opposed to each other. They were rather twin doctrines, each finding its one genuine antithesis and opponent in Marxism. Where liberalism had been the characteristic doctrine of a capitalist free-market economy to which all state intervention was alien, totalitarian—by which Marcuse meant Nazi or Fascist—thought was characteristic of a capitalist free-market economy which, in order to subjugate criticism and to prevent action to abolish the economy, had had to invite the state to politicize the whole of life.

It is clear that Marcuse was influenced in adopting this view by the personal intellectual history of a number of the key figures in European thought. Gentile, the Italian idealist philosopher, had written to Mussolini that "liberalism as I understand it, the liberalism of freedom through law and therefore through a strong state, through the state as ethical reality, is represented in Italy today not by the liberals, who are more or less openly your opponents, but on the contrary by you yourself," and he had joined the Fascist Party. Heidegger, who had passed from Husserlian phenomenology to existentialism, joined the Nazi Party and as a university rector proclaimed to his students, "Let not doctrines and 'ideas' be the rules of your being. Today and in the future, only the *Führer* himself is German reality and its law."

Marcuse saw Gentile and Heidegger as representative figures: that tradition of philosophical thought which in the seventeenth and eighteenth centuries had been at once rationalistic and optimistic had now become identified with irrationalism. Instead of the universalism which envisaged *man* as the subject of philosophy, one had particularist doctrines of race and nation, rational criticism of which was to be prevented by the subordination of reason to the forces of blood and soil. Marcuse's writings in the years from 1933 to 1938 are dedicated to the defense of what he takes to be the rationalist core of earlier European philosophy against contemporary irrationalism. In trying to understand this defense we shall also have to understand Marcuse's concept of philosophy.

When Marcuse wrote about the history of philosophy his perspective was a peculiarly German one. The Greeks and especially Aristotle received a lot of attention; the Middle Ages very little. Descartes was important and then Kant, who prepared the way for the philosophical climax achieved by Hegel. After Hegel, apart from Marx, attention was paid to Husserl and to Heidegger. Positivism and empiricism appeared usually as very general and imprecise doctrines, of which the Vienna Circle was the main representative, only in order to be rejected. In all this Marcuse was at one with the mainstream of German academic philosophers. But in accepting that the great philosophers are Aristotle, Kant, and Hegel, Marcuse interpreted their greatness in a particular way of his own. The essential function of philosophy, he argued, was *criticism* of what exists. Philosophy was able to provide us with an account of the structure of thought in particular times and places because it also provided us with a standpoint which transcended the limitations of particular times and places and of particular structures of thought. Marcuse has never denied that the practice of philosophy was historically conditioned, but the distortions imposed by that conditioning were less at some periods than at others; one therefore found in the history of philosophy periods in which philosophical thought had the power to transcend its immediate environment.

We can clarify this view of philosophy further by contrasting it with that of Marx and Engels. Engels in 1888, looking back to the period forty years earlier when he and Marx had elaborated their materialist conception of history, argued that this conception "puts an end to philosophy in the realm of history, just as the dialectical conception of nature makes all natural philosophy both unnecessary and impossible." What Engels meant was that both history and nature had now been liberated from a study which viewed them only through the medium of distortions. Instead the course of history and of nature could not be studied directly. Engels allowed that logic and what he called "the laws of thought" remained within the province of philosophy. But he believed that the claims of philosophy to afford a substantive view of the nature of reality had finally been discredited. Indeed, he and Marx had shown the history of philosophy, to be very, very largely part of the history of ideology, he believed, of those forms of thought which are secondary to, derivative from, and a reflection of a basic economic and social reality.

The characteristic which had led Marx to this view of philosophy was its abstract quality. In *The German Ideology* he made fun of Hegel's abstractions. In the *Economic and Philosophical Manuscripts of 1844* he saw the Hegelian philosophy as depicting, but only in a misleadingly abstract form, the concrete human condition. And in his later writings the abstract was always the detrimental. Not so for Marcuse. For him, it was—and indeed is—the detachment of philosophy from what is concrete and immediate which gave it power. Just because philosophy was concerned with concepts, with the structure of what *can* be thought, it confronted the realm of actuality with that of possibility. In different periods it did so in different ways. But the history of philosophy did not concern only those philosophical concepts which were culture-bound, which belonged to one age and not to another; even those metaphysical concepts which were apparently most unvarying differed from period to period in their relationship to each other, in their place in the conceptual scheme, and also in their relationship to concrete actuality.

We can illustrate what Marcuse meant by this by considering certain episodes in the modern history of the concept of essence as he traced it in a paper in 1936. Marcuse contrasted modern writers with their predecessors from Plato to Hegel, who used the concept of essence to make a distinction between the true nature of things and things as they merely happen to be at any given moment, between what is authentically real and what only appears as such. Such writers, in Marcuse's view, made a valid distinction between things as they are and things as they could and should be. This distinction was not made in the same way in ancient Greece, by Aquinas, and by the philosophers of the seventeenth century, but some version of it was always made. When, however, one encountered modern phenomenology in the person of Husserl, one found a crucial difference. Husserl claimed to be redoing the work of Descartes, and he did draw a distinction between essence and existence. Phenomenology, in studying what is presented to consciousness, became the study of essences; it was part of the meaning of everything belonging to the world of fact, of everything contingent, "to have an essence and thus an *eidos* that is to be grasped in its purity." Phenomenology thus grasped the essences of things by abstracting their mere facticity, their mere belonging to the spatio-temporal world. But precisely because the phenomenologist arrived at his abstractions by beginning from what is, he renounced the notion of any fundamental contrast between actuality and possibility. The phenomenologist's account of possibility was, in Marcuse's view, necessarily a mere reproduction at another level of a world of actuality presupposed by his whole mode of operation. Husserl claimed it as a merit for phenomenology that it aimed to be descriptive in its method. Marcuse saw it as condemned to being merely descriptive. While maintaining the distinction between essence and existence, phenomenology had in fact deprived this distinction of its most important function.

If phenomenology was thus written off, positivism received even shorter shrift. In Husserl's claim to be descriptive, Marcuse saw the baneful influence of positivism on phenomenology, for he took it to be positivist doctrine that no distinction between a realm of essence and a realm of actuality can be made. The positivist he cited was Moritz Schlick: "There is no fact that compels or even justifies us in making such a contrast between two irreducible realities." So Marcuse characterized the positivist position himself: "With respect to knowledge, all facts are as such equi-valent. The world of facts is, so to speak, one-dimensional."[1] When Schlick criticized the doctrine of two realms of Being by saying, "One kind of Being is considered higher, more genuine, more noble and more important than the other, i.e. an evaluative conception has been introduced," Marcuse did not disagree, but he believed that this was legitimate and that Schlick considered it a criticism of the doctrine only because he made a false distinction between fact and value. "Positivism adheres to the bourgeois ideal of presuppositionless, pure theory, in which the absence of 'ethical neutrality' or the commitment of taking a position signifies delinquency in rigor."

In contrast to phenomenology and positivism Marcuse praised Marxist materialism. Precisely because Marxist materialism both envisaged a contrast between what man happens to be at the moment and what man could become, and also distinguished between how things really are in a capitalist society and the false consciousness that men in such a society possess, it restored the concept of essence to a central place. We are thus not limited to things as they are; in the light of Marxist materialism "given facts are understood as appearances whose essence can be comprehended only in the context of particular historical tendencies aiming at a different form of reality." Essential structures are revealed by historical development; the realm of es-

[1] *Negations* (Boston, 1968), p. 65.

sence is not a static, timeless, Platonic realm, but a realm which consists in showing how at any one moment the facts only partially and one-sidedly reveal the structures in the light of which they can be understood. Moreover, this knowledge of historical structures is what gives us a basis for the criticism of existing reality. "The theory's historical interest enters constitutively into its conceptual scheme and makes the transcendence of 'facts' towards this essence critical and polemical."[2] We criticize what *is* in the light of what *could be*, and we identify what *can be* by our knowledge of historical tendencies, of what *will be*.

In Marxist materialism, "connecting at its roots the problem of essence to social practice restructures the concept of essence in its relation to all other concepts by orienting it toward the essence of *man*."[3] The essence of man is, in Marcuse's view, an ideal informing our present practice and guiding it toward the goals of a new form of social life which will be "the real fulfillment of everything that man desires to be when he understands himself in terms of his potentialities."

Marcuse's account of the history of philosophy in the modern age is situated within a more general account of the history of modern culture. Two features in this culture are central. The first is the transition from a period of affirmation in the early bourgeois age to a period of resignation and denial. In the period of affirmation a sharp distinction developed between the mental and spiritual world on one hand and the material world on the other. The world of the mental and spiritual was essentially inner; it made unconditional claims upon the individual, superior to those made by the material

[2] Ibid., p. 71.
[3] Ibid., p. 72.

world; and the individual was called upon to transform himself in accordance with them. This transformation was possible, even though the material world remained untransformed. "In bourgeois poetry, lovers love in opposition to everyday inconstancy, to the demands of reality, to the subjugation of the individual and to death."[4] But in everyday life love is not what bourgeois romanticism makes it, but what bourgeois economy makes it, a thing increasingly of duty and habit.

This intensifying rift between the inner and the outer world was characteristic of bourgeois culture. As it intensified, so there was an intensified need to express in terms of the "inner" what could no longer find a place in external social life. The concept of the soul in its romantic version became the concept of that portion of the personality which strives to fulfill necessarily unexpressed and unachieved desires. The soulless regions were the regions of material life; the soul sought an ideal beauty and an ideal happiness which could not be real. When finally the bourgeoisie could preserve their social and economic order only by politicizing it through and through, and by subjecting the individual wholly to the demands of that order, then this inner realm, in which the individual had preserved a small area of private freedom from the external demands of bourgeois life, must come under attack. Hence the new totalitarians had to attack the culture of the bourgeois past in order to preserve the economic order of the bourgeois present.

The second main theme in Marcuse's analysis of the history of modern culture concerned the relationship of freedom to happiness. According to Marcuse, freedom and happiness were intimately connected. "Happiness,

[4] Ibid., p. 111.

as the fulfilment of all potentialities of the individual, presupposes freedom . . . at root, it is freedom." Because moral philosophers both in the ancient world and in the bourgeois period recognized the impotence of man in respect to his external environment, they rejected any notion of a pleasure dependent on environmental circumstances as the—or even a proper—goal for men. The circumscribed notion of freedom in the bourgeois period led to an even more circumscribed notion of happiness. Moreover, in bourgeois society enjoyment was connected with the individual's limited freedom from the necessity of work and of the market. Enjoyment was bound up with the notion of leisure and was so devalued. This devaluation was never more radical than in connection with sexuality. Spinoza, speaking of sensual pleasure, wrote that we may "indulge ourselves with pleasures only insofar as they are necessary for preserving health." Fichte wrote that it would be "absolute dishonor, the abnegation of authentic human and manly honor," if man's capacity "as original progenitor to produce out of himself new men" were "made into a means of sensual pleasure." Procreation in Fichte's period still served the end of bourgeois marriage. When the bourgeois society becomes authoritarian and totalitarian, the same divorce between procreation and pleasure is maintained, and procreation now serves the ends of the state, the production of workers and soldiers.

There was in fact another important respect in which, according to Marcuse, bourgeois society could not allow for happiness. It was that bourgeois society was unable to reconcile particular happiness with general happiness. A society which enforced work-discipline of a kind that was tolerable only when man was induced to value work for its own sake, and in which the social order was exploitative, competitive, and therefore divisive, had to repress and channel the desire for pleasure toward limited individual ends, whereby it often became a source of frustration and destruction. By contrast, "the unpurified, unrationalized release of sexual relationships would be the strongest release of enjoyment as such and the total devaluation of labor for its own sake." This release would make individuals conscious of their total lack of satisfaction in the work-process and so make them cease to tolerate the bourgeois social order. Equally, so long as the bourgeois social order existed, sexuality must be frustrated.

These ideas were formulated by Marcuse in a number of papers published between 1934 and 1938 in the *Zeitschrift für Sozialforschung*, the journal of the Institute of Social Research, which had emigrated from the University of Frankfurt to Columbia University in New York. Marcuse taught for a year in Geneva in 1933–1934 and then went to New York to join the Institute, where he was a colleague of its founders, Max Horkheimer and T. W. Adorno. The importance of these early papers is not only that they constitute a first statement of the thesis which informs the whole of his later work. For on certain points they are more explicit than anything in the later work. They also stand in a somewhat different relationship to Marxism. It is therefore worth while to pause at this point in the exposition of Marcuse's thought in order to raise some critical questions which may also illuminate further the nature of Marcuse's enterprise.

Some Critical Questions

11

Criticism of Marcuse's positions encounters two kinds of difficulties; those posed by particular theses which he asserts, and those posed by his whole manner of thought and style of presentation. Marcuse's manner is both literary and academic; he is allusive and seems to presuppose in his readers not only a high level of general culture but a wide area of presumed agreement on academic matters (such as the interpretation of Descartes, to give only one example). This manner was one developed as part of the culture of the professoriate in imperial Germany. It does not invite questioning, but suggests that the teacher is delivering truths to the pupil which the pupil has merely to receive. It is less offensive in English translation than in its German original, if only because its very strangeness lends to it a certain charm.

This manner inevitably involves a difficulty of substance. Marcuse seldom, if ever, gives us any reason to
believe that what he is writing is true. He offers inci-
dental illustrations of his theses very often; he never
offers evidence in a systematic way. Above all, there is
entirely absent from his writing any attempt on his own
part to suggest or to consider the difficulties that arise
for his positions, and hence also no attempt to meet
them. But, of course, from the fact that Marcuse tends
to substitute assertion for argument and to offer no
reason for believing that what he says is true, it does
not follow that what he says is false. I shall raise four
initial questions.

The first arises from the issue which I have just
raised. Marcuse at various points both in his early and
later writings refers to criteria of truth which he rejects. What is Marcuse's own view of truth? He does
not make it clear what criteria of truth he accepts or to
what criteria of truth he is appealing when he invites
us to accept his assertions. And in what he does have to
say about truth two subordinate difficulties arise. Marcuse contrasts what is true with what is merely actual,
and rejects as empiricist any notion of truth as corre-
spondence with fact, since in his view to be limited to
the facts as they are is to be delivered over to untruth.
But in so doing he never tells us how we are to determine what the facts actually are; yet his interpretation
of the history of culture is itself true or false depend-
ing on what the facts are. Moreover, all discourse and
argument depend on the participants' mutual acceptance of common criteria of truth and rationality. When
in philosophy these criteria are themselves the subject-
matter of rational debate, it is all the more important

to be explicit about how one takes the truth on these matters to be determined.

The question is sharpened by the second subordinate difficulty. Marcuse sometimes writes as if each age had its own criterion of truth—a position which at the very least is not inconsistent with certain other positions he holds. But if truth is relative to time and place, how can we judge between theories which belong to different times and places? The need for an impersonal, non-relative concept of truth is clear.

My second critical question is: how does Marcuse justify his highly selective version of the history of culture? This question can be broken down into parts. First, how does Marcuse justify his highly selective version of the history of philosophy? The omissions are evident. Locke and Berkeley, Diderot, Helvétius, and d'Alembert never appear, Hume scarcely ever; Spinoza and Leibnitz get very short shrift; Nietzsche is in, but not Schopenhauer; Schlick but not Mach. Why is this important? The answer is that by omitting so much and by giving a one-sided interpretation of those authors whom he does invoke, Marcuse is enabled to exaggerate, and in some instances to exaggerate grossly, the homogeneity of the philosophical thought of a given age. I do not deny that often we may perceive in the most diverse and competing philosophical doctrines shared lineaments which indicate membership in a common culture and perhaps presupposition of a common world-view. But that this is so in a given period has to be *established*.

If Marcuse's history of philosophy is dubious, his general history of culture is even more so. For one thing, he appears too much to read the history of culture through lenses provided by his own version of the history of philosophy, and for another, he does not even use literary evidence adequately. We have an interesting contrast in Lucien Goldmann, to take another Marxist writer. According to Marcuse, the early bourgeois age (unlocated in place for the most part) is one of rationalism and optimism; Descartes is the paradigm figure. According to Goldmann, in France that age was deeply marked by a tragic view of life, and Descartes must be viewed in the perspective provided by Pascal. It is unfair to match Goldmann against Marcuse— Goldmann's thesis is much more solidly based in every way than Marcuse's—but to suggest the comparison draws attention to the arbitrariness of Marcuse's writing of history.

My third critical question concerns Marcuse's correlation of philosophical doctrines with political and social commitments: how is this correlation established? Certainly not by any actual correlation between a philosopher's doctrines and his commitments on such matters. Marcuse sees phenomenology and empiricism as doctrines characteristic of a world passing into totalitarianism, and in his early writings what Marcuse means by totalitarianism is the authoritarianism of Fascism and Nazism. But in fact the philosophers of the Vienna Circle were radicals and socialists, anti-Nazi to a man, and the political record of the phenomenologists was also good. (Edith Stein, Husserl's secretary, became a nun and died in a concentration camp.) Heidegger and Gentile were, in fact, highly exceptional figures. How, then, is Marcuse justified in treating them as representative ones?

Suppose it is answered that the connection between philosophical doctrine and social or political stance is an inner conceptual connection, that Marcuse is charging not that those who hold certain doctrines are more likely to have certain attitudes, but that the doctrines themselves are somehow or other appropriate to such attitudes. Everything would then turn on being able to specify what the criteria of appropriateness were. It is not impossible that this should be achieved for certain doctrines. For example, it appears to be the case that liberalism as a political and moral doctrine depends on a notion of the individual as sovereign in his choice of values. The facts do not and cannot constrain such choice, but the free individual is determined by nothing but himself. For this to be so there must be discernible in the language that we speak a class of factual statements and a class of evaluative statements whose relationship is such that no set of factual statements can separately or jointly entail an evaluative statement. At the same time liberalism clearly is at home only in, its contentions are intelligible only against a background of, certain types of historical and social setting. Thus a logical doctrine about fact and value might indeed be rooted in a more general moral and political doctrine, which in turn presupposed the background of a certain type of society. But we would be entitled to make this assertion only if we had worked out in detail what I have sketched in briefly and cryptically; and equally certainly we would be entitled to hold a more general position about the connection between types of philosophical theory and types of social structure only if we had done this in a substantial number of cases. Marcuse's arguments on particular points do in fact presuppose that this has already been done. It has not.

The fourth critical question is: how does Marcuse's view stand in relation to classical Marxism? We cannot assimilate Marcuse's thought too easily to Marxism even at this stage of his development. For one thing, there is the distinctive view of the power of philosophy which I have already noted. He sometimes speaks not of Marxist materialism but of "the critical theory of society," and the point of this seems to be not only an ambiguity common to the utterances of his Frankfurt colleagues, but also a very proper insistence of his own that, if he identifies himself as a Marxist, we must be careful to understand what *he* means by "Marxism." But what, apart from his rejection of any too easy view of culture and philosophy as mere ideology, does Marcuse advance that is distinctive? It is difficult to say, because his utterances on, for example, economic questions amount simply to *assertions* that Marxist economists have analyzed the historical tendencies of a capitalist economy successfully. Thus Marcuse's doctrines are at this stage underpinned by a commitment to Marxism the extent of which cannot be gauged from the writings. Politically he did pin hopes to the Soviet Union and to the Spanish republic's struggle against Fascism; but nothing more specific than this very general form of political commitment informs his writing.

There is, however, one other point in which he differs strikingly from Marxism not by profession but by practice. It is connected with his view of philosophy, for it concerns his willingness to rely upon abstractions. Marcuse is endlessly willing to talk of "man" rather than of men, of what "man" desires or does or suffers. Here we do well to be reminded of Marx's remark in *The Communist Manifesto* where he compares certain German thinkers with those monks who wrote lives of the saints on top of classical manuscripts: "The German literary pundits reversed this process with the profane French literature. They wrote their philosophical nonsense behind the French original. For instance, behind the French criticism of the economic functions of money, they wrote 'elevation of humanity,' and behind the French criticism of the bourgeois state they wrote 'dethronement of the category of the general,' and so forth." Indeed in *The German Ideology* Marx attacks Feuerbach precisely because "he says 'man' instead of 'real, historical men'" and he attacks both Feuerbach and Grün for speaking of "the essence of man."

Is the resemblance between Marcuse and the Left or Young Hegelians whom Marx attacked superficial? Is it only a matter of style and phraseology? Marx's accusation against the Left Hegelians was not that they were Hegelians but that, instead of transforming Hegelian theory so that it became a guide to the empirical realities of contemporary society, they used it as a series of abstractions through which they could view contemporary society only in distorted form. Part of this distortion was, in Marx's view, to exaggerate grossly the causal effectiveness of theorizing by itself as an agency for changing society. Do these charges in any way apply to Marcuse? Examination of the early writings of 1934 to 1939 suggest that they might and that we ought at least to consider the hypothesis that Marcuse is not a post-Marxist but a pre-Marxist thinker who has regressed to just that practice of "criticism" (the Left Hegelians used the same word) which Marx criticized. In considering such a hypothesis nothing could be more important than examining Marcuse's interpretation of Hegel. To this I now turn.

Marcuse's Interpretation of Hegel and Marx

● ● ●

iii

In 1941 Marcuse published *Reason and Revolution: Hegel and the Rise of Social Theory*. He begins in characteristic fashion by connecting Hegel's philosophy with the French Revolution, but in this case Marcuse is not open to the criticism I have advanced of some of his other attempts to connect philosophy and politics. For it was, after all, Hegel himself who first insisted upon this connection. It was of the French Revolution that Hegel spoke in his lectures in Berlin on the philosophy of history when he said "Never since the sun had stood in the firmament and the planets revolved around it had it been perceived that man's existence centers in his head, i.e. in thought, inspired by which he builds up the world of reality. Anaxagoras had been first to say that *nous* [mind] governs the world; but not until now had man advanced to the recognition of the principle that thought ought to govern spiritual reality. This was accordingly a glorious mental dawn. All thinking beings shared in the jubilation of that epoch." But if in Hegel's view the realization that reality is the construction of thought first came to consciousness in action in the French Revolution, it first came to consciousness in philosophical form in Hegel's philosophy; and Hegel was prepared to see in the enunciation of his own philosophy a companion world-historical event.

To elucidate the relationship between Hegel's thought and the age of and immediately following the French Revolution, I shall first give a necessarily highly compressed outline of Hegel's philosophy, indicating the points at which there are crucial disputes about its interpretation. Then I shall look at Marcuse's place among the interpreters of Hegel. And finally I shall ask what Marcuse took from his study of Hegel into his own thought and more particularly what he carried from his study of Hegel into his interpretation of Marx.

Kant had argued that we are able to understand the world and to know truths about it only because the mind brings to its task of understanding a set of categories by means of which it organizes what is given in experience. Experience never comes to us raw, but mediated by the categories. We experience things as having determinate qualities and relations, because the conceptual structure which thought imposes on the world gives determinate form to what would otherwise be formless. Moreover the categories of the understanding are fixed once and for all; the mind itself has a determinate, unchanging constitution.

Hegel began by accepting from Kant this central insight—that we take the world to be as it is because the

structure of thought imposes a structure on it—but then
he wished to quarrel with the Kantian position in two
respects. For Kant, there was a distinction to be made
between reality-as-we-apprehend-it and reality-as-it-is,
between things-as-perceived and things-in-themselves.
The latter are and will be unknowable. But, argued
Hegel, if they are unknowable we cannot know of them
and we cannot know that they are; hence we must conclude that reality simply is reality-as-we-apprehend-it.
There is nothing beyond and outside experience. But
Hegel did not further conclude that claims which have
hitherto been understood to concern realities that cannot be experienced—God, the minds of others—are all
false; rather we must understand these claims instead
as claims about the character of certain features of the
world as we experience it. Hegel was a consistent anti-
dualist.

Second, Hegel attacked the notion that the categories
are timeless and unalterable. The history of thought is
a history of changing conceptual structures. Elucidating the categories of a given age must not be confused
with elucidating the structure of thought as such. To
elucidate the structure of thought, a history has to be
written, a history exhibiting growth both in consciousness and in self-consciousness. For it is by becoming
conscious of their present mode of thought that men are
able to criticize it and rationally to transcend it. The
end and culmination of such a history would be the
rational comprehension of the whole process, which in
that culmination would be seen as the completion of
reason, a point at which knowledge that was absolute in
a new sense would have been achieved. Hegel's philosophical writings represent successive attempts to write
and rewrite that history; but there is only one book in

which he attempted something like the complete history of human reason: the *Phenomenology of Mind*, written in 1806 in Jena and finished—so the traditional, but possibly apocryphal, story runs—with the sound of Napoleon's guns at the Battle of Jena in his ears. Since that battle marked the ascendancy of the post-Revolutionary Napoleonic regime not only in France but in Europe as a whole, the moment has an important symbolic quality.

The *Phenomenology of Mind* is many things. It is a history of philosophy in which Hegel not only reviews the main philosophical positions of the past but attempts to depict exhaustively the range of philosophical positions which are possible. (And how extraordinarily impressive his attempt to carry out this impossible task is, is shown by the way he anticipates philosophical positions which were only to be worked out in the future by his successors and critics. There are, for example, recognizable sketches of Kierkegaard's existentialism and Russell's logical atomism, and refutations of them too.) But since for Hegel the thought-forms which the philosopher discerns are those which inform civilization and not merely philosophical theorizing, the *Phenomenology* situates the history of philosophy within a history of the human spirit. Art, politics, religion all pass in review. The pattern which informs all of these is one that Hegel elaborated in the course of reflecting upon the contrast between the ancient Greek city-state and the Germany of his own age.

Hegel in some of his most youthful writings saw in the Greek *polis* a form of human community in which the individual found his identity within the political community and thought of the state not as an alien power set over him but rather as his true home; and in which politics and religion were not distinct and contrasted activities so that the individual had one set of earthly ties and another, more ultimate heavenly allegiance which might separate him from those to whom his earthly ties bound him. In the modern world the individual and the state were at odds, partly because of the historical effect of the Judaeo-Christian tradition, which in giving men a sense of infinite possibility and goals had led them to see their citizenship of the earthly city as secondary to their citizenship in heaven. To recover the lost unity of human nature, the finite and the infinite must be reintegrated, and Hegel came to see this recovery as the goal of history, an idea implicitly informing patterns of historical development.

Men move from earlier forms of unity to later forms of disunity and then to a reintegration on a higher level. They do so by moving outward from themselves to see the world as objective and given and independent of human reason, and then to understand that it is reason that makes both man and his world what they are. Hence the task of philosophy is to make man at home in the world again. The process of objectification has also been one of alienation. Men have come to view things which are in fact products of their own activity, which are sustained in being only by their own activity —such as morality and the state—as alien and oppressive powers with a life of their own. The coming of reason into its own involves abolishing alienation. It is now possible to see why Hegel believes freedom and reason to be intimately connected: the conditions for men communally to truly understand their history and their present situation are identical with the conditions for men to be rid of all false dependence either on the external world or on each other. To be free is to have learned what can and what cannot be altered. To be rational is to have recognized freedom as the goal of history.

Every age is an *ensemble* of human relationships, a totality with its own conceptual structure and institutional arrangements. In saying this, Hegel's position might appear to resemble that of later theorists in sociology and anthropology, for whom societies and cultures are systems of interlocking parts, each part contributing to the maintenance of the whole system. On the contrary, Hegel believed that every set of social forms contained discrepancies and contradictions; that each embodied incompatible principles such that to work out the potentialities of a given society and culture was always to breed explicit contradiction and conflict and to bring about its transformation into something else.

Consider, for example, some of Hegel's characterizations of the pre-Revolutionary society of the eighteenth century. It was, on one hand, an individualist society, guided by the maxim that each shall pursue his own happiness. But where this maxim was installed as a social norm, where men attempted to specify a whole way of life in terms of this maxim, we encountered a contradiction. For the man who wills his own happiness is also being asked to will that every other man shall will *his own* happiness, yet the other who does this becomes for him an obstacle and an enemy. This conflict called forth solutions in the realms both of theory and of social institutions. In the realm of theory, utilitarian philosophers appealed to sympathy as a motive and to the notion of the greatest happiness of the greatest number. In the realm of institutions, there was a counterpart to the individualism of civil society in the pre-

Revolutionary state which repressed and regulated in a way that claimed to represent not particular interests but the general interest, and yet did so in a manner that was necessarily arbitrary from the standpoint of every individual.

Both types of solution were themselves necessarily incoherent. The very irreconcilability of the pursuit of his own happiness by each with the same pursuit by others, which set the problem of harmonizing interests, made it impossible to sum happiness and posit as a joint goal the happiness of all or even the greatest happiness of the greatest number. For this goal conflicted with the individual's goals just as much as did the goals of other individuals. Equally, because there was no general interest, the state could not really represent it but could only pretend to and in so doing work its function of protecting some particular interests, namely the interests of the privileged and ruling class. Consequently, instead of being a solution to the conflicts of individualism, the *ancien régime* state was itself an obstacle to freedom and reason and in this name was overthrown. Robespierre proclaimed, in words which, as Marcuse has noted, Hegel perhaps self-consciously echoed, that "the power of reason, and not the force of weapons, will propagate the principles of our glorious revolution," that "all fictions disappear before truth, and all follies fall before reason."

But Hegel also recognized that the Revolution had not only created its own fictions and follies but defended them by force of weapons, by terror. It had done so because it represented and was itself infected with the individualism of civil society to such an extent that in relation to institutions it could only be destructive and negative, it could only see social order as a barrier to freedom. What the social forms were which might transcend the competitiveness of individualist civil society and realize freedom positively, Hegel left obscure in 1807; later he was to contrast the positive order inspired by Napoleon with the negative drive to freedom of the Revolution. "The world-spirit on horseback," said Hegel of Napoleon; the abolition of a thousand petty jurisdictions and arbitrary princely wills, the institution of the *code Napoleon*, the creation of civil equality, the revocation of ecclesiastical privileges—these were the kind of measures that Hegel saw as introducing rationality in place of irrationality in social institutions.

Yet if Hegel was prepared to see in Napoleon both a sequel to Robespierre and a more adequate political counterpart to his own philosophy, it remains true that the status of his own age must present an acute problem for Hegelian philosophy. For in Hegel's philosophy reason had become truly self-conscious at last, aware of the entire history of its own development and thus achieving its own culmination and completion. The Absolute Idea realized itself in rational form; this is why Hegel was only being consistent when he wrote in the *Logic* that his pen was writing the thoughts of God. But since the history of philosophy is only a part of the history of the self-development of the Idea, since it is only a central thread in the total history of culture and institutions, the institutions of Hegel's age must manifest the self-development of the Idea in the same way. If the conditions of reason's final emergence were satisfied, the conditions for freedom's final emergence must have been satisfied too. If Hegel's philosophy was itself indeed the emergence of reason, where was freedom?

Hegel's own answers to that question changed. In

turn he considered the Jacobins, Napoleon, the claim that after Napoleon's defeat the philosophers must temporarily withdraw from the political scene, and the Prussian monarchy. Hegel accepted the competitiveness of civil society as part of the necessary order of things: only the state could transcend particular interests, and only the state could therefore represent true rationality in institutions. The arguments Hegel advanced to show that the Prussian monarchy of the post-Napoleonic settlement was the true representation of the rational state were so feeble that detailed criticism pays them an undeserved compliment. We ought to note, however, that Hegel's account of the culmination of history was obscure and enigmatic not only at the political but also at the philosophical level.

The *Logic*, where Hegel sets out the form of the Absolute Knowledge in which rationality culminates, is a study of the categories of the mind in their development and interrelationship. Its central lesson lies not in the details of Hegel's scheme of categories, but rather in his assertion that the application of no set of categories is self-justifying; that we can always stand back and ask for an account of how such an application is possible and why it is justified; that the concepts we use to give such an account can in turn be put to the question and transcended in the same way. So, in dealing with the category of Quantity, Hegel points out that whenever we apply mathematics to a subject-matter and whenever we formalize our arguments and theory, the justification of the mathematization and formalization must always be in some other terms. Hence philosophical justifications which must be required and given for any procedure, formal or otherwise, must be metalogical and so evade the requirements of formalization:

"It must be a mere refuge of philosophical impotence when it [philosophy] flies to the formations which logic takes in the sciences." Thus the relation of Hegel's logic to formal logic and mathematics is not one, in Hegel's own view, of rivalry; there is no claim that formal reasoning is invalid or inapplicable. Rather, Hegel held that philosophical argument about the possibilities and limits of formal reasoning cannot be *a priori* limited by appeal to the rules of formal calculi.

What, then, is the character of philosophical reasoning? Hegel's continual plea is that we do not try to separate formal truths from substantial ones. The concepts with which we reason are neither such that their meaning and criteria of application are fixed once and for all nor such that shifts in meaning and criteria can ever be arbitrary. It is in the context of the growth of actual knowledge that the Notion takes on its life. Philosophy is thus in the end identical with science, for we cannot study the concepts of a given science independently of knowing what the truths of that science are. Insofar as philosophy has a more specific function, it is that of providing a synthetic review which transcends those conceptual schemes and theories that are at home only in particular sciences.

This summary outline of Hegelianism enables us to inquire into Marcuse's interpretation of Hegel. Marcuse becomes critical in other than the most marginal way only when he turns from Hegel's *Logic* to his political philosophy. He sees the root of Hegel's error in his political acquiescence in the existing order after 1815; he sees not the content of Hegelian theory but its application to political life as being at fault. We may observe at once that this is very much what some of the

Left Hegelians held at one stage. But the question that
has to be raised sharply is whether in fact the *content*
of the Hegelian philosophy—and that content which
Marcuse on the whole refrains from criticizing—does
not lend itself to political aberration. We may approach the answer to this question by considering Marcuse's position on two standard questions of Hegel
interpretation.

The first concerns the relation of the categories of the
Logic to the empirical material to which they apply.
Here two related points are relevant. Commentators on
Hegel tend to divide into two parties: one stresses that
the categories are antecedent to nature and to history
and that the self-development of the Idea through the
categories is specified in terms of relations between the
categories themselves; while the other stresses that this
antecedence is only logical and not temporal, and that
the categories have no existence apart from their em-
bodiment in the world of experience. Hegel's own
pupils divided on this issue immediately after his
death. For the Right Hegelians, who took the former
view, the Absolute Idea could never be reduced to its
temporal and finite manifestations; for the Left or
Young Hegelians, to take this view was merely to re-
store the theistic dualism of God and the World which
Hegel had sought to abolish. Hegel himself was genuinely ambiguous, but I do not want to ask which view is
correct so much as to point to the corresponding attitudes to Hegel's writings. Those who take the Right
Hegelian view naturally enough treat the *Phenomenology* as a not wholly mature work, an anticipation of
the more systematic *Logic*. Those who take the Left
Hegelian view tend to see the *Logic* as a misleadingly

abstract exercise, apt to leave the impression of a fixity and a finality in the scheme of the categories which Hegel in fact at his best had wanted to deny.

What is fascinating here is that Marcuse's account of Hegel does take the *Logic* with extreme seriousness. He does not treat the obscure and enigmatic treatment of the culmination of rational progress at the end of the *Phenomenology* as a sign that Hegel's argument has somehow gone astray. Instead he says firmly, "The foundations of the absolute knowledge that the *Phenomenology of Mind* presents as the truth of the world are given in Hegel's *Science of Logic*." But this is to read the earlier work in the light of the later, to view the more concrete in the light of the more abstract. It is to ignore how much of what Hegel does say is empirical.

Of history Hegel wrote in the Preface to the *Phenomenology* that, as far as the purely historical element is concerned, it had to do with matters of contingent fact, and it is clear that he believed them to be the subject of empirical inquiry. It is also clear that his attitude to the physical sciences was the same. Now just because, as Marcuse puts it, "dialectical logic links the form of thought with its content," and just because, as Hegel insists, we cannot deduce the contingent content from the form, Hegel can set out the forms of thought as he does only on the basis of a broad empirical view of human development, which is implicitly introduced. The assertions of the *Logic* can be true, that is, only if certain empirical theses are also true. This connection of the forms of thought with the empirical is perceived by Marcuse, but, like Hegel himself in some passages—although only in some passages—he views it upside-down. "For," Marcuse asks, "what does the unity

of identity and contradiction mean in the context of social forms and forces? In its ontological terms, it means
that the state of negativity is not a distortion of a
thing's true essence, but its very essence itself. In socio-
historic terms, it means that as a rule crisis and col-
lapse are not accidents and external disturbances, but
manifest the very nature of things and hence provide
the basis on which the existing social system can be
understood."[1] But this is precisely to admit what I have
just asserted, that the Hegelian scheme, even when
presented in terms of the most extreme abstraction, has
a covert empirical content. It follows that the question
of whether the Hegelian scheme does or does not apply
to the actual world is an empirical question. This question Marcuse never asks. He therefore accepts without
any critical examination the same view of the actual
world that the late Hegel did. What this view amounts
to can be better understood if we turn to Marcuse's
position on a second question of Hegel interpretation.

The Hegelian notion of the Absolute carries with it
the notion of a point at which history is in effect complete and the whole historical process can be comprehended within a scheme of categories which no longer
stand in need of revision. The philosophical exposition
of these categories, as I have already noted, Hegel took
to be what his own work in the *Logic* consisted in. In
his political philosophy Hegel was rightly unwilling to
carry this absolutizing, this deification, of the present
to the same lengths. Although the Prussian state was in
his view the actual state which approached most nearly
to rationality and therefore to being a final expression
of the Idea, Hegel was careful not to place Prussian
institutions beyond criticism. He did, however, increas-

[1] *Reason and Revolution* (Boston, 2d ed., 1954), p. 48.

ingly endorse monarchical and anti-liberal sentiments, and Marcuse detects in his tendency to do this a retreat into a hitherto uncharacteristic pessimism. This pessimism coexists uneasily with the generalized optimism of the *Philosophy of History*, according to which historical change is "an advance to something better, more perfect," for Hegel certainly did not see all the changes in his own time as such advances.

Yet what Marcuse attacks is only Hegel's attitude to contemporary development; he leaves unassailed the whole notion of the Absolute, and he therefore leaves open the possibility of absolutizing and deifying tendencies in the present other than those which Hegel approved. In fact when Marcuse passes from the interpretation of Hegel to that of Marx, what he does is to endow Marx's analysis of bourgeois society and capitalist economy with features which properly belong to Hegel's account of the realization of the Absolute Idea. He does this partly by not distinguishing Marx's more Hegelian periods and work from his less Hegelian ones. *The Economic-Philosophical Manuscripts, Capital, The German Ideology*, and *The Contribution to the Critique of Political Economy* are all drawn upon in a single exposition of Marx's view of the place of labor under capitalism, as though Marx had a single and unchanging doctrine which is expounded in all these works. The Marxist doctrine which Marcuse expounds makes it clear why Marcuse is so surprisingly uncritical of the Hegelian Absolute. For Marcuse accepts in substance Hegel's view that the history of philosophy does culminate with Hegel. Hegel completes philosophy; and Marx inaugurates a mode of thinking in which the limitations of philosophy are overcome and a mode of thought is discovered which enables us to transform not merely thought, but social reality. Thus the Hegelian characterization of Hegel's own age as that in which the dialectic of history reaches its culmination, this characterization which absolutizes and deifies the Hegelian present, is transferred to the characterization of the climax of capitalism in Marxist terms. The Absolute is come among us; but it is disclosed not in the closing sections of the *Phenomenology* but in *Capital*.

Marx, on Marcuse's interpretation, produces a doctrine which is the final achievement of consciousness in history, or rather prehistory, in two senses. For not only, as I have just noted, is philosophy now transcended, but the class structures of society which produced the alienated labor have also developed to the point at which they can be transcended. This latter possibility Marcuse expounds, purporting to be reporting Marx but in fact using a Hegelian vocabulary which Marx and Engels had abandoned by 1846. (We may note that the counterpart to Marcuse's Hegelianizing of Marx is a total neglect of Engels as an authentic interpreter of Marx.) "Every fact is more than a mere fact; it is a negation and restriction of real possibilities. Wage labor is a fact, but at the same time it is a restraint on free work that might satisfy human needs. Private property is a fact, but at the same time it is a negation of man's collective appropriation of nature." The word "negation" is being used here, as is the word "restriction," so that it makes both an uncontentious logical point and a contentious political one. For every fact is a negation and restriction of real possibility: if it is the case that it is raining, then it is not the case, it is the negation of the case, that it is not raining. If one possibility is realized, others, for example that it is dry or that it is snowing, cannot be. But Marcuse also means that what is prevented from being the case by the facts being as they are is something that would increase human freedom; and in meaning this he is true to Hegel. Yet Marx did abandon the practice of merging the logical and the evaluative in a single vocabulary. Indeed Marcuse quotes a passage from *The German Ideology* where Marx mocks at the Hegelian terms "the Higher Being" and the "Notion" in a way that suggests that he might have been equally willing to mock at "Negation." So that to expound Marx without mentioning this change is misleading; it is not enough to say as Marcuse does that "Marx's early writings are mere preliminary stages to his mature theory, stages that should not be overemphasized."

But if Marcuse carries over into his analysis of Marx's mature writings Hegelian ideas that do not properly belong there (some Hegelian ideas do properly belong there; Marx did retain, even if he also modified, the notion of alienation, contrary to the view of such interpreters as Lewis Feuer), he at the same time oddly ascribes to Marx a break with Hegel that Marx did not make. I have already noticed that Marcuse connects freedom and happiness intimately. He argues that the Hegelian progress of reason is not a progress to happiness and says, obviously correctly, that Marx took human needs far more seriously than Hegel did. But he then passes from asserting that for Marx a truly human and free society would be one in which each would have the possibility of realizing his potentialities (and that this is what Marx means by freedom) to asserting that "mankind becomes free only when the material perpetuation of life is a function of the abilities and happiness of associated individuals."[2] And he characterizes part of the difference between Hegel and Marx by saying that "the idea of reason has been superseded by the idea of happiness."

It is important that Marcuse does not produce a single quotation from Marx to support this view. Marx had castigated the view of happiness adopted by the utilitarians; and had he wanted to adopt the notion of happiness as a human goal, he would surely have said so. Some later Marxists have certainly been utilitarians —Kautsky was. But most have been clear that freedom is a goal which may be incompatible with the goal of happiness. Trotsky's view that the gap between aspiration and achievement will be a permanent feature of human life, so that tragedy will be permanently relevant to contemporary human experience, seems far more faithful to Marx's view than Kautsky's was. And on this point Marx and Trotsky are surely right and Marcuse surely mistaken.

The acceptance of freedom as a goal is the acceptance of the possibility that in utilizing their freedom men will produce situations which invoke frustration, sacrifice, and unhappiness. Marcuse believes that for men to be satisfied they must be free; but clearly in any ordinary sense of "happiness" or "satisfaction" men may be more easily satisfied or happy when certain possibilities have not been opened to them. A developed talent for musical performance or literary composition may well be the source of endless pain and dissatisfaction. Hence Marcuse's notion of happiness at this point is an arbitrary intrusion and a gratuitous falsification of Marx.

[2] Ibid., p. 293.

A distortion that is, if possible, even more important occurs when Marcuse discusses Marx's view of the transitions to socialism and then to communism, transitions which both Marx and Marcuse see as a passage from the realm of necessity to the realm of freedom. But Marcuse, having acknowledged that Marx did envisage the transition from capitalism to socialism as law-governed, and predictable precisely because law-governed, argues that "it would be a distortion of the entire significance of Marxian theory to argue from the inexorable necessity that governs the development of capitalism to a similar necessity in the matter of transformation to socialism." Marx himself presumably is included among those who have distorted the entire significance of Marxism. For Marcuse has just quoted Marx as writing in the first volume of *Capital* that "capitalist production begets, with the inexorability of a law of Nature, its own negation," which he characterizes as a society founded on a basis of "cooperation and the possession in common of the land and of the means of production." Marx did believe, that is to say, that both social life under the reign of necessity and society's transition to freedom are law-governed; Marcuse cannot believe this because he equates the realm of necessity with that area of social life which is governed by laws and he takes it to be a necessary condition of free action that its course should not be so governed.

This position Marcuse asserts, as he asserts so many positions, unargued. But it is of course a position that has often been held. For if we can show that an action has cause in the sense of sufficient antecedent conditions which either singly or collectively produce the action as an effect, then it follows that once the event(s) or state of affairs which constitute the cause have occurred, then the action which is the effect had to occur, could not have not occurred. Thus it appears that if an action is in this sense caused, it is not free. But if an action is correctly explained by invoking a law or a lawlike generalization to the effect that "whenever an antecedent event or state of affairs of such-and-such a kind occurs, then an action of this kind will occur," then that action is clearly caused in the relevant sense. Hence the argument has been advanced that if an action is law-governed, it is not free.

If this is the argument that underlies Marcuse's position, it is highly dubious. For when we count an action unfree or non-rational, as we do the compulsive behavior of neurotics, we do so if the action is outside the agent's own rational control, if it cannot be altered in the light of relevant deliberation. But for this to be the case it is not enough that the action be caused; the causes of the action must be such as to render the agent incapable of rational control, irretrievable to rational considerations. If the agent's own rational deliberation *is* the cause of his action, this is a paradigm case of free and rational action. Hence it is not, as Marcuse supposes, whether an action is or is not caused and law-governed that matters; it is the character and the content of the causes and the laws in question.

Marcuse's position in this matter dominates his interpretation of later nineteenth-century thought. The fundamental antithesis is between Marx and Hegel on the one hand and the tradition of positivism on the other. But the essential content of positivism which Marcuse rejects is the assimilation of the understanding of society to the natural sciences in respect to their logical structure. Natural science is for Marcuse a form of knowledge distinct from and apparently perhaps even inferior to that provided by dialectical theory. In judging this to be the case Marcuse is once more at variance both with Marx and with Engels. But, more important, his own position is made implausible. For the point of dialectical theory, on Marcuse's account, is to exhibit those possibilities which men could realize, but which are not realized by present social arrangements. Now, the knowledge of what is actually possible is the knowledge of what kinds of properties, what kinds of events, and what kinds of states of affairs do as a matter of fact coexist and must coexist, and which do not and cannot. For if the laws governing the relevant area are such that one property, or type of event, or kind of state of affairs is related to another in such a way that either both must occur or the occurrence of one excludes the occurrence of the other, then certain combinations of properties, events, or states of affairs are possible and others are not. That is to say, what is possible depends upon which statements of laws or of lawlike generalities turn out to be true; and this is so with human as with natural possibilities. Hence the knowledge of future human possibility depends upon the knowledge of which laws will govern future human affairs. But from this it follows that Marcuse's central thesis about the future collapses into incoherence. And this is surely not unimportant.

Why Marcuse distinguishes the knowledge of human society from the knowledge of nature in the way he does and why he consequently adopts the attitudes he does both to the interpretation of Marxism and to positivism are matters which deserve further consideration. But they can be raised more adequately in the context of an assessment of *Soviet Marxism* and *One-Dimen-*

sional Man. With those works we shall also have to pass from the question whether Marcuse is a faithful interpreter of the Hegelian and Marxist traditions to asking even more insistently whether what he says— whether faithful to Hegel and Marx or not—is true.

It is already, however, strikingly clear that Marcuse's attitude to Hegel and Hegelian theory is not the attitude of Hegel himself nor is it that of Marx. The hypothesis that it is with the Left or Young Hegelians that Marcuse should be classified is reinforced by the way he treats Hegelian theory and even its Marxist version as providing us with a standard of rationality against which the actual world must be judged. Marx in *The German Ideology* described the intellectual fate of those who did this. Marcuse's subsequent writings confirm Marx's diagnosis.

Freud Reinterpreted:

Eros and Civilization

●

IV

I have in the course of the preceding argument picked out certain positions which distinguish Marcuse from other writers in the Hegelian and Marxist traditions to which he owes so much. More especially I have suggested that in making "man" rather than "men" the subect of history he is at odds with Marx, and that in making "happiness" a central goal of man's striving he is at odds not only with Hegel, as Marcuse himself recognizes, but also once more with Marx. It is perhaps because of these differences that Marcuse has found it possible to be in many respects a Freudian as well as a Marxist when most Marxists have been extremely critical of and antagonistic to psychoanalysis. Not all, of course; Trotsky was profoundly interested in psychoanalysis, but what seems to have engaged *his* interest was primarily psychoanalysis as a method of therapy rather than Freud's metapsychological theory. For Marcuse it is all too characteristically the other way round. With Freud's own writings it is continually necessary for the reader to turn back from the theorizing to the case histories, from the inflated conceptual schemes to the revealing clinical detail or other shrewd empirical observations; and it is in such observations that in the end the evidence for the truth or the falsity of psychoanalytic claims must be found. Marcuse is as impatient of the empirical here as he is elsewhere.

Freud, like Marcuse, envisaged man, a unitary human nature, as seeking a goal of happiness, in the search for which frustration and defeat have continually ensued. But, unlike Marcuse, Freud was concerned to explain certain empirical phenomena, notably the symptoms of neurotic patients. He introduced the concept of unconscious motivation in the first instance to explain the occurrence of hysterical paralysis, a disorder in which the area paralyzed corresponds not to the objective physiological facts, but to the patient's beliefs about his own physiology (something of which the hysterical patient is himself quite unaware). Any plausible explanation of neurotic behavior would of course contain an account of what it is that differentiates the neurotic patient from the normal man and would to that extent also involve a theory of normal behavior. So Freud came to advance a theory of human development as such and then to apply his theory in a not always systematic fashion to art, religion, and politics. It is worth emphasizing that, as Freud moved in this direction, he moved from more or less empirically controlled theorizing to what was necessarily almost pure speculation, and that where there is empirical evidence in the fields about which he speculated it often does not support his hypotheses. Yet it is precisely into this speculative area that Marcuse follows Freud, an area in which criteria of truth and falsity are inevitably more difficult to apply. Hence in assessing what Marcuse says we are involved in initial difficulties of the first order.

Yet it is clear why Marcuse should have found it urgently necessary to enter this particular area of inquiry. When Marx envisaged the period of transition from capitalism to socialism, he seemed to forecast two processes which would go on side by side. One was the economic breakdown of the capitalist system, and he predicted the course of this with some clarity: the relationship of mechanization to human labor changes, the limits of market expansion are reached, tendencies toward monopoly intensify, the rate of profit falls, the ability to recover from slumps decreases. The other process was the growth in political consciousness of the working class. About this Marx said much less. He envisaged the concentration of workers in large factory units and the limits set upon the growth of wages as necessary conditions for the growth of this consciousness; but he said nothing about how or why the workers would learn and assimilate the truths which Marxism sought to bring them. This lacuna in Marx's thought, this failure to provide a social psychology, allowed some vulgar Marxists to suppose that the growth of working-class consciousness would be some kind of automatic reflex of the same economic processes that produced the downfall of capitalism. This was neither Marxist nor true. Indeed one might write the history of the period from 1848 to 1929, an age which Marxism illuminated much more clearly than any other doctrine did, as one in which Marx's view of the progress of capitalism was substantially correct, but at the end of which, when the Marxist script for the world drama required a European working class to emerge as the agent of historical change, the working class turned out to be quiescent and helpless.

The suggestion therefore that under capitalism men are dominated and exploited not merely by external oppressors, by those who own and those who rule, but by forms of consciousness which prevent them from liberating themselves is very much to the point for someone concerned from a generally Marxist standpoint with the events of 1929 and after. But it may seem paradoxical that Marcuse should have turned to Freud to supply the social psychology that Marxism lacks, since Freud's own political views, both as citizen and as theorist, were highly conservative. It has been conjectured that while a young man in Paris, Freud acquired his fear of the politics of the masses; certainly a contrast between civilization on one hand and the masses on the other was part of the ideology of French conservatism, nourished as it was on fear of the Revolution and even more of the Commune, which reappears in Freud's writings.

According to Freud, the biologically founded basic instinctual drives of human nature are controlled and repressed in the interests of the internalized authority of the parental figures, the superego, and in those of the ego, the self which seeks to preserve its integrity in the face of reality by mediating between the rival claims of instinctual forces, of id, and of superego; ego has also to mediate between the rival claims of the drive for pleasure, which is instinctual, and an external reality in the face of which this drive must be disciplined and repressed. But it is not only the individual who, by repressing his instinctual desires, wins an area of conscious ego control. Civilization is founded on this very process of repression. It is by an ascetic renunciation of instinctual pleasures that libido is made available in sublimated form for the tasks of creating high culture. Only a minority elite are able to engage in these tasks; were they to lose this control of the social order, the blind instinctual passions of the masses would destroy civilization.

For Freud, therefore, the theory of society is founded upon two contrasts, that between freedom and happiness and that between sexuality and civilization. The contrast between freedom and happiness is founded on the premise that liberation is essentially liberation from the hold that the instinctual desires of infancy and the fixations resulting from the encounter of those desires with the external world still have upon us. But such liberation depends upon the ego, with its grasp of the reality principle, displacing from its sovereignty the instinctual id, with its commitment to the pleasure principle. "Where id was, there ego shall be." So the pleasure principle cannot govern the life of the free individual. But according to Marcuse, as I have already noted, the connection between freedom and happiness is both conceptually and empirically so close that unless Freudian theory can be detached from this contrast, it would seem impossible that he should be able to make use of it.

For precisely the same reason, Marcuse has to reject the contrast in Freud's writings between sexuality and civilization. For Marcuse the works of culture can be, and as a matter of fact have been, achieved by sexual renunciation. But the connections between sexuality and happiness on the one hand and the culture he wishes to see and freedom on the other are so close that Marcuse has to show that sexual and other social relationships are not so different as Freud supposes. Freud envisages any social order larger than that between sexual partners as founded on a common, enforced, unrecognized renunciation of sexual life. Marcuse wishes to envisage a possible social order in which human relationships are widely informed by that libidinal release and gratification which, according to Freud, would spell the destruction of any social order.

Since Marcuse wishes to assert that the history of civilization has been very much as Freud described it, he must and does argue that the contrasts between freedom and happiness and between sexuality and civilization are the outcome of specific institutions which belong to particular stages of human development and not the outcome of human nature as such. The two concepts he introduces to emend Freud's account are surplus repression and the performance principle.

By "surplus repression" Marcuse means a set of restrictions which are necessary if some particular form of social domination is to be maintained. He distinguishes it from "basic repression," that set of restrictions upon the instincts necessary, for the reasons given by Freud, to found and to maintain civilization. Marcuse takes it to be true that a certain basic repression and asceticism were indeed necessary to build civilization because of economic scarcity and the work necessary to overcome it. But the form of the distribution of resources, whether meager or increased by the effort of work, and the form of the organization of work have always been imposed upon men, and the forms of repression necessary to maintain them represent an overplus beyond what is necessary for civilization. Furthermore, as technical and material progress removes the obstacles which scarcity placed in the path of civilized development, repression is more and more surplus to the task of maintaining civilization and more and more a matter of maintaining specific and removable forms of social domination.

To the claim that it is the reality principle which demands repression Marcuse retorts that we confuse the demands of the reality principle with the demands which some particular form of social domination seeks to impose in the name of reality. That we should perform our social tasks in an allotted order and hierarchy is not a prescription of reality as such; the principle embodied in this prescription is what Marcuse calls the performance principle.

Marcuse uses these two notions of surplus repression and the performance principle to argue that human history can be divided into two phases. In the first, which has lasted until the modern age, social domination was necessary to remove scarcity and lay the technological foundations for abundance; but now the repression of the energies of sexual libido and their expression only in the controlled forms of work and of the limited monogamic sexuality of the socially required family is needlessly repressive. Human liberation requires that sexuality should not have to express itself any longer in the form of a social order it cannot recognize as its own, that is, from which it is alienated, but must liberate itself from this false renunciation and asceticism. Sexuality is thus for Marcuse something which must be liberated if man is to be liberated. What would be the differences in the character of sexual behavior if sexuality was to be liberated?

Since Marcuse sees the channeling of sexual libido

into genital and monogamic channels as part of the process of surplus repression, he consistently sees at least some of the taboos imposed on forms of sexuality taken to be perverse as part of the irrational apparatus of repression. "The same taboo is placed on instinctual manifestations incompatible with civilization and on those incompatible with repressive civilization, especially with monogamic genital supremacy." In a culture where this is no longer so, a self-regulated sexuality will regress from a state where it is generally controlled in the interests of reproduction to one where the goal of "obtaining pleasure from the zones of the body" (Loewald) having been restored, the whole body becomes involved and "the field and objective" of the sexual instinct become "the life of the organism itself."

It would be wrong to blame Marcuse himself entirely for the comic pomposity of his discussions of sex, which are dominated by the principle "Never use a four-letter word where a twenty-four-letter word can be found," because he is merely following a well-established psychoanalytic tradition and using a well-worn psychoanalytic vocabulary. But it is impossible to avoid asking Marcuse, as he picks his way through allusions to coprophilia and nervously glances at sadism: "What will we actually *do* in this sexually liberated state?"

It is not enough to answer that the potentialities of human sexuality in a liberated state cannot be foreseen. For the notion of an unrepressed or at most self-sublimated and liberated sexuality has no content until some answer is given; what is worse, the notion that contemporary sexuality is constrained by the limitations of monogamic, genital sexual culture has no content either, until some contrast with what is possible but unrealized has been effectively delineated. Marcuse's failure here is fatal to his whole argument. Once again the failure is related to his lack of interest in empirical facts. Marcuse revises Freud in the interests of his own theory; but he apparently takes it for granted that a Freudian account of sexuality is not fundamentally defective, and he makes no attempt to inquire independently what the facts about sexuality are. It is scarcely surprising that his treatment of rival and incompatible theories verges on the scandalous. No psychoanalytic writer has done more to explain what a liberated sexuality might be and what the contrast between an unliberated and a liberated sexuality consists in than Wilhelm Reich; and no psychoanalytic writer identified himself with the struggle against Nazism more than Reich did. One might therefore have expected a sympathetic and careful account of the differences between Freud and Marcuse on the one side and Reich on the other and a consideration of what empirical tests would be decisive in determining on which side, if either, truth lies. Instead, Reich is dismissed in twenty-one lines culminating in a sneer at "the wild and fantastic hobbies of Reich's later years," simply on the grounds that his views differ.

Reich, for example, rejected Freud's hypothesis of the death instinct; Marcuse accepts it but does not mention that almost all those acquainted with the relevant empirical facts agree with Reich in rejecting it. Marcuse sees the death instinct at work in the destructiveness of modern technology and more especially in that destructiveness which "reveals time and again its origin in a drive which defies all usefulness. Beneath the manifold rational and rationalized motives for war against national and group enemies, for the destructive conquest of time, space, and men, the

deadly partner of Eros [that is, Thanatos, the death-
instinct] becomes manifest in the approval and partici-
pation of the victims."[1] Let us for the moment waive
the question whether it is true that the victims of modern war approve of and participate in their own destruction and attend instead to this passage as one which
poses the question of how far Marcuse has been in fact
successful in reconciling his neo-Marxist theory with
his neo-Freudian.

Both Marx and Freud concern themselves with the
explanation of certain types of unintended consequences
of human actions. The Freudian explanation invokes
the notion of unconscious wishes which produce outcomes either not consciously intended by the agent or
inconsistent with his consciously formulated and sin-
cerely avowed intentions. A characteristic example is
the slip of the tongue, where what was intended to be
uttered as a respectful salutation emerges as an insult
or a joke. But large and complex patterns of behavior
toward others may be explained in a similar way. When
Marx is concerned to explain unintended consequences,
he does so by appealing to the character of the social
structure the agent inhabits, and the agent's blindness
to it. Men produce consequences they do not intend because they are ignorant of the causal laws governing
economic relationships and because they do not perceive that the working of the whole economic system, at
least in modern society, depends on men's failing to
understand the relationship of their decisions to the
larger structures. It is the independence of the workings of the economy which leads men to see society as
an alien power and which alienates them from it. Nobody wills, or at least nobody need will, the destruc-

[1] *Eros and Civilization* (Boston, 1954), p. 52.

tive outcomes of a modern capitalist economy; the destructive outcomes are precisely the result of an uncontrolled economic system which does not embody human motives or wishes. Hence Marx insists in the Preface to *Capital* that his indictment of capitalism assigns no responsibility to the individual capitalist.

The notion of alienation can be extended, and is extended by Marx (for example in the 1844 manuscript), far beyond the sphere of economic relationships; and the notion of unconscious sexual wishes can be extended, and is extended by Freud and by many Freudians, beyond the sphere of personal relationship into that of economic activity. But at first sight it is a difficult question whether these modes of explanation are incompatible or not. It is at least clear that if we could explain the occurrence and destructiveness of modern war by referring to the workings of the economic system (as in fact we cannot), we should not need to invoke unconscious destructive instinctual drives to explain the same phenomena. But perhaps the phenomena are overdetermined? Perhaps both causal agencies are at work? To ask this question and even to suggest the difficulty of answering it is to bring to light a feature which both modes of explanation have in common. They are both too general to function as genuinely explanatory notions. To explain the occurrence and the character of modern war, for example, we need to be highly specific; no explanation will be adequate which does not explain why wars occur here rather than there, now rather than then, and so on. But since, on the neo-Marxist view which we are considering, all the characteristic features of the dominant social order are part of the phenomena of alienation, nothing is *explained* by invoking alienation. It does not, of course, follow that we do not have other, descriptive uses for Marx's concept of alienation.

Equally, since Thanatos is supposed to be at work in all human destructiveness, it cannot explain the particular character of any highly specific destructive phenomena such as those of modern war. There is in addition the problem of how we are to identify the presence of the death instinct independently of its manifestations, which we must be able to do if we are to treat one as a cause of the other. It is indeed precisely this type of difficulty that has discredited the concept of Thanatos.

Yet if the difficulty in using the concepts of alienation and Thanatos for explanatory purposes means that the question of how their explanatory use can be reconciled is superfluous, it is still true that Marcuse's joint use of these concepts raises another type of difficulty. For Marx the question of the general character of the social order and that of the fate of individuals were inseparable, and explanatory primacy belonged to the former; for Freud social phenomena were to be explained in terms of the characteristics of individual human nature. Marcuse is able to disregard the fundamental nature of Freudian individualism because he is willing to identify the development of the individual and the history of past society so completely. Every individual's development recapitulates the history of the race. This is a doctrine which it is difficult to make sense of except as an elaborate and fanciful metaphor. If, for example, one argues, as one would have expected Marcuse to do, that a changing technology has a key part in the history of society, what counterpart is there to this in the development of the individual? Such difficulties can obviously and easily be multiplied, and

Marcuse's approach ignores them. "The replacement of the pleasure principle by the reality principle is the great traumatic event in the development of the genus (phylogenesis) as well as of the individual (ontogenesis). According to Freud, this event is not unique but recurs throughout the history of mankind and of every individual. Phylogenetically, it occurs first in the *primal horde*, when the *primal father* monopolizes power and pleasure and enforces renunciation on the part of the sons. Ontogenetically, it occurs during the period of early childhood. . . ."[2]

So Marcuse makes the recapitulation thesis depend on the resemblance between a set of events in prehistory and a set of events in infancy. It is therefore at the very least surprising that it turns out to be irrelevant to Marcuse whether the prehistorical events actually happened or not. He allows that the "archaic events that the hypothesis stipulates may forever be beyond the realm of anthropological verification,"[3] but insists that the hypothesis has "symbolic value." By this Marcuse seems to mean that if we interpret the facts of later human history *as if* Freud's hypotheses about the primal events were true, we can understand them better. How we would test this contention is unclear, but once again the question is superfluous because of a prior difficulty.

Freud's account of the primal horde is a social-contract story designed to explain the origin of social institutions. The primal father monopolizes the women —and so pleasure—and subjugates the sons. The sons hate the father and combine to kill and eat him. United by guilt at parricide, they form a clan with taboos

2 Ibid., p. 15.
3 Ibid., p. 60.

against parricide and incest which are self-imposed. They no longer struggle to succeed to the position of the father, for they understand that this is futile. This leads to "a union among them, a sort of social contract. Thus there came into being the first form of a social organization accompanied by a renunciation of instinctual gratification; recognition of mutual obligations; institutions declared sacred, which could not be broken —in short, the beginnings of morality and law."[4]

Even if, with Marcuse, we wish to treat this account not as a true historical narrative but as an *as if* story, an illuminating metaphor, it is necessary that the account be internally coherent. What embodies a contradiction cannot function successfully even as a metaphor. Yet Freud's account is internally incoherent and self-contradictory. As in Hobbes's account of the social contract, it has to be explained how the transition can have been made from a condition in which the relations between men were purely those of force, in which each sought to impose his own will on others, to a condition in which there were socially established norms and institutions which regulated human behavior in an impersonal fashion. The stages by which this transition was made are not the same as in Hobbes's account; they are guilt, the establishment of taboos, and the making of a social contract. But each one of these presupposes the prior existence and functioning of just those social norms and institutions the origin of which they are to explain.

Guilt is a response to a breach of what is taken to be a recognized norm; it is not just strong negative

[4] Sigmund Freud, *Moses and Monotheism* (New York, 1955), p. 129.

feeling. To make something taboo requires established institutional arrangements; in a situation in which *ex hypothesi* the only established forms of practical utterance are expressions of personal will, how could such institutional arrangements exist? A contract cannot be made except when the institution of promising and norms regarding promise-keeping are established. Thus the allegedly primal state is not pre-institutional, pre-legal, or pre-moral at all. It follows that it cannot function in Freud's narrative as Freud intended it to or as Marcuse requires it to.

This failure makes the whole recapitulation thesis in its Marcusean form untenable. But it could still be the case that, although Marcuse's version of Freud is inapplicable to the human past, it is illuminating about the potentialities of the human future. Marcuse asserts that it is in fantasy that our allegiance to the pleasure principle is preserved—in play, in dream, in daydreaming—and that it is in works of the imagination that we find the most visible "return of the repressed" and the anticipation of new forms of human life in which our sexuality is transformed and libido informs all our human and work relations. These relations will be no longer relations of domination, and hence surplus repression will be at an end. But what will social relationships of this kind be like? How will they differ from present social relationships? It is scarcely enough to characterize them in terms only of the not wholly clear notion of libido and the absence of domination. Marcuse equates them with a condition in which man will achieve his free self-realization, but he also allows that men will still have different needs and different modes of satisfaction and that conflict would continue.

Why would these conflicts not lead to new forms of domination? On this Marcuse is silent, and perhaps he is silent because his account is in fact empty.

It is worth noting, finally, that in *Eros and Civilization* too, Young Hegelian themes recur. The project of explaining human culture as involving the alienation of man from his sexuality, of seeing Eros at the heart of human things and alienation in the forms under which Eros is apprehended and encountered, is essentially Feuerbach's. Some trace of Feuerbach's view is to be found in some of Marx's earliest writings, in one passage in *The Poverty of Philosophy*, for example. But Marx, following Hegel in relating alienation to work, turned his back on Feuerbach's anticipations of Freud. In reviving them, Marcuse again suggests to us that he is not a post- but a pre-Marxist thinker. This hypothesis ought to receive its severest test in *Soviet Marxism*, where Marcuse adopts a Marxist point of view more explicitly and at greater length than anywhere else in his writings. I shall therefore pass on to inquire whether even in his professions of Marxism, Marcuse succeeds in ridding himself of his pre-Marxist standpoint.

Soviet Marxism

V

Marcuse's study of Soviet Marxism in the years 1952–1953 and 1955–1956 was necessarily a study of Stalinist and immediately post-Stalin Marxism. It suffers from the same defect as his work on Western society: it is curiously bare of actual facts about Russia. But it is, after all, unlike *Eros and Civilization*, which preceded it, and *One-Dimensional Man*, which was to follow it, by intention the study primarily of a doctrine rather than of a society. The introduction to *Soviet Marxism* contains some important, if obscure, remarks by Marcuse about his method. Marcuse explicitly disowns a Hegelian perspective, if that implies that history is to be interpreted teleologically. But how much of Hegel does he disown in disowning this? In *Eros and Civilization* Marcuse had once again treated Hegel's thought as the culmination of

Western philosophy. The tradition in Western philosophy which culminates in Hegel is one in which—on Marcuse's interpretation—reason sets up standards to which empirical reality must conform if it is not to be irrational. Hegel supposes that not only as a matter of fact has empirical reality in the course of history come closer and closer to meeting the requirements of reason, but because the course of history is actually the progress of the idea, a progress informed by reason, empirical reality must in the end satisfy these requirements as closely as possible. Marx, however, saw that this teleology involved Hegel in a falsification of modern history and saw too that the task of making reality rational has now become practical and possible. On the basis of industrialization, men—or rather the working class, since they alone of mankind are not bound to the existing order and to past history—can and must remake the social order in accordance with the requirements of practical reason.

The Soviet Union in the early nineteen-fifties was a society for which its official representatives claimed that this task of construction had been in progress for over thirty years. Marcuse's critique is based on the certainly correct claim that what has happened in Soviet society is not that social reality has increasingly conformed to the requirements of theoretical Marxism, but instead that Soviet Marxism has been increasingly adapted to fit in with the requirements of Soviet reality. More than this, Soviet Marxism has altered the whole framework within which Marxism is to be understood. The formulas of classical Marxism are now used not to state truths but to instruct in a conformist practice. "Taken by themselves they are no more committed to the truth than are orders or advertisements: their 'truth' is in their effect."[1] Marcuse characterizes the utterances of Soviet Marxists in a variety of ways: as pragmatic, as incantatory, as magical. We necessarily see this whole mode of practice as irrational, but "what is irrational if measured from without the system is rational within the system."[2] Marcuse has therefore two tasks: to reconstruct the internal coherence of Soviet Marxism and then to criticize it in the light of its departures from classical Marxism. We can consider his treatment of Soviet Marxism in terms of four key examples.

Stalinist aesthetics insisted that literature and painting should portray Soviet reality in naturalistic fashion, viewing it in an optimistic light, and the reality of the non-Soviet world equally naturalistically, but pessimistically. Art must be naturalistic because its function is to depict the facts as they are. Marcuse contrasts this Soviet view with Hegel's view that art belongs to a period in which the difference between the ideal and the actual is such that art, committed to the manifestation of the ideal, is essentially non-naturalistic; Hegel seems to claim that the realization of the ideal would in fact leave art functionless. Soviet Marxism, in claiming that the ideal is being realized in Soviet society, takes away from art what Hegel—and Marcuse—believe to be its function. Soviet aesthetics "wants art that is not art and it gets what it asks for." Marcuse insists that the state's direction of art is not the root of the trouble; it is rather the doctrine which informs that direction. But what is most striking about his discussion is its lack of

[1] *Soviet Marxism* (New York, 1958), p. 88.
[2] Ibid., p. 86.

social concreteness. He never considers, for example, that academic naturalism is a doctrine that has appeared in other times and places, notably in Victorian England—another society dominated by a technically oriented, sexually conservative bourgeoisie. By insisting on judging Soviet society in its own terms, by restricting himself to what he calls an "imminent critique," he produces an enormously parochial impression.

On the Soviet doctrine of the Soviet state Marcuse stresses that, according to Marx, the state belongs not to the economic basis of society but rather to the superstructure. In capitalist and pre-capitalist society, therefore, the economic basis determines the form of the state and the state cannot control economic change. But according to Stalinist doctrine the state has now become the agency which directs and controls economic change. The state power will not wither away so long as the Soviet state confronts both external and internal enemies. But those who run the state and share in state power, the bureaucracy, have no separate economic basis which gives them a long-term interest distinct from the interests of the Russian people as a whole. So Stalinist doctrine. Marcuse, on the contrary, insists that the bureaucracy has developed divisive special interests. He does so on the basis of the following generalization: "Bureaucracy by itself, no matter how huge it is, does not generate self-perpetuating power unless it has an economic base of its own from which its position is derived, or unless it is allied with other social groups which possess such a power base." Marcuse then argues that the Soviet bureaucracy through its control of a nationalized economy does have such a power base, but unfortunately he has given us no reason to accept his initial generalization.

What is at stake here? An alternative hypothesis might be, for example, that a bureaucracy first acquires a special interest and generates a self-perpetuating power without having any specific common *economic* interest, but that it may then secondarily acquire such an interest. A key case in which we should be deciding between the claims of these two rival hypotheses would, of course, be just that of the history of the development of the Soviet bureaucracy. But Marcuse never brings his generalization to the test of history, nor indeed to any other test. He reads Soviet history rather in the light of his own Marxist generalization.

The theory of the state is in any case perhaps one of the more difficult parts of Marxism for Marcuse to apply his method to. Marx is notoriously unspecific about the details of the transition to socialism and about how precisely staᴖe power will be exercised during this transition. Marcuse, however, takes it that Stalinism totally misrepresents Marx on these matters because it fails to understand the basic character of the transition. This accusation Marcuse bases on his understanding of Marx's doctrine of dialectics. Stalinist Marxism envisaged the laws of dialectics as high-level causal generalizations governing all change, whether physical or social. It follows that the transition to socialism is law-governed, but just this, as I have already noted, Marcuse denies. For Stalinism the transition from necessity to freedom is itself law-governed; for Marcuse it is not. There is no need to repeat the discussion, in the third chapter of this book, of Marcuse's doctrine on this point; but we certainly ought to note that if Marxism has changed its point of view on this subject it had already done so by the time Engels wrote on this topic in *Anti-Dühring* and read what he had written to Marx. When a Stalinist philosopher wrote in 1955 that "under socialism, too, the laws of the social development are objective ones," it is far from clear that he was falsifying Marx. Marcuse, in quoting from M. T. Iovchuk, italicizes the phrase that follows this assertion, "operating independently from the consciousness and will of human beings," but is even this phrase false to Marx's intentions? Marcuse admits that Engels and Stalin substantially coincide in their views of dialectics. If he insists that even Engels is false to Marxism, is he not under an obligation to offer some evidence of a disagreement between Marx and Engels on this matter? Or is *even Marx* false to Marxism here?

The truth of the matter, as we have already found reason to believe, is that Marcuse has composed a new amalgam of fragments of Hegel, Marx, and others and called it "Marxism" in *Soviet Marxism*. It is as if when the old Marx said—as he did once—that he at least was not a Marxist, Marcuse retorted, "Indeed—but I am." Marcuse's version of Marxism is false to Marx not only in its content but in its whole treatment of the relationship between Marxism and social reality. When Marcuse indicts Soviet Marxism for its disagreement with what he takes to be Marxism, he supposes that the history of the Soviet Union in its negative aspects is to be explained without reference to Marxism. Marxism remains as a theory pure and uncontaminated, providing a standard by which Soviet reality can be judged. Marcuse's account of the Soviet Union is thus at the opposite pole from the views of those who suppose that it is from Marxism that all the evils of Soviet reality spring and who see in the transition from Marx through

Lenin to Stalin an entirely unproblematic development. But if this latter view is clearly absurd—Marx was throughout his career a radical democrat, who believed that all that was wrong with the liberties of bourgeois parliamentary regimes was that their enjoyment was effectively restricted to a minority—it will not do to treat Marxism as a theory that can be evaluated apart from its historical fate. To do so would in any case be completely contrary to Marxism.

Both Marcuse and Soviet Marxists agree with Marx that at the point at which the transition from capitalism to socialism takes place the relationships that have held between different social institutions are transformed. It becomes possible to direct social change in ways that have hitherto been impossible, and this means that, even if Soviet Marxists can be indicted for their view of the function of the state in this transition, it is common ground that impersonal economic forces lose their dominant place in the causal chains of history. It follows that to this period the analysis of types of human social activity into basic and superstructural can no longer apply in the same way that it has previously. One consequence of this will presumably be that those who carry through the transition—the working class and their political representatives—will be able to think objectively about society and be free of the constraints hitherto exercised by the false consciousness of class society. They will be free from ideological deformation. But if this is so, then Marxism as it actually exists cannot be the theory of this transitional period, just because it is in fact subject to the kind of ideological deformation which Marcuse identifies.

Lukàcs argued in *History and Class Consciousness*

that historical materialism had to learn to turn its method on itself. If the claim of historical material- ism—that every theory is marked by features which belong to it because it was generated in some particular type of economic and social order—is true, then his- torical materialism itself must be marked by such fea- tures. Lukacs argued in particular that the distinction between the economic—which is basic—and the politi- cal—which is superstructural—in Marxism derives from the separation of the economic from the political in bourgeois societies in which the state does not inter- fere with the workings of a market economy; but his point has many further applications. On a Marxist view, any theory which can be exhibited as having the history that it has because of its ideological function in social orders can be understood only by some other theory which grasps the original theory from outside and is able to place it in its historical context, so rel- ativizing it and viewing it as necessarily distorted in some of its features. On Marcuse's view, Marxism can be exhibited as having this type of history. It follows that Marxism too must now be viewed from the outside as a necessarily distorted and distorting theory. It would be inconsistent with Marxism itself to view Marxism in any other way; in particular, we must not try to judge and understand Marxist theory as it has really existed with all its vicissitudes in the light of some ideal version of Marxism. It follows that, by the present time, to be faithful to Marxism we must cease to be Marxists; and whoever now remains a Marxist has thereby discarded Marxism.

It follows further that there are no Marxists—what- ever men may think themselves. But if Marcuse is not a Marxist, what then is he in his use of ideal Marxist theory against actual Marxist theorizing? The answer has been given already. To judge the actual inadequate in the light of idealized theory is at the heart of Young Hegelianism. In *Soviet Marxism*, once more Young Hegelianism is resurrected. It turns out, alas, to be senile.

One-Dimensional Man:

The Critique of Contemporary Society

vi

One-Dimensional Man marks a sharp break in Marcuse's thought, even though the substance of his thesis about Western industrial society is already to be found in *Eros and Civilization*, and that about Soviet society in *Soviet Marxism*. What is new is twofold: his virtual relinquishing of any distinctively Marxist—as against Hegelian—categories, and his pessimism. In *Reason and Revolution* Marcuse had reproached Hegel for his final relapse into pessimism—Hegel looked forward with apprehension to the developments he saw foreshadowed in the British Reform Bill of 1831 —"Hegel's philosophy ends in doubt and resignation." Nobody could justly accuse Marcuse of resignation, but there is surely at least doubt expressed in the 1960 preface to the third edition of *Reason and Revolution* when Marcuse speaks of "a mental faculty which is in danger of being obliterated: the power of negative thinking." Since, according to Marcuse, negative thinking is the sole source of creative social criticism, he in fact fears the obliteration of creativity in social life. This fear provides the theme of *One-Dimensional Man*.

The central oddity of *One-Dimensional Man* is perhaps that it should have been written at all. For if its thesis were true, then we should have to ask how the book came to have been written and we would certainly have to inquire whether it would find any readers. Or rather, to the extent that the book does find readers, to that extent Marcuse's thesis does not hold. For Marcuse's thesis is that "technical progress, extended to a whole system of domination and coordination, creates forms of life (and of power) which appear to reconcile the forces opposing the system and to defeat or refute all protest in the name of the historical prospects of freedom from toil and domination." Even thought has been subordinated so that it provides no source for the criticism of social life. If social control in the interests of the *status quo* is then so powerful, how has Marcuse's book evaded this control?

Marcuse's answer is given in his introduction. He holds that there are forces and tendencies in society which now run counter to the tendency that his book describes. He asserts that *One-Dimensional Man* is concerned with these counterforces and tendencies also; but they do not, except for one or two paragraphs, appear in his book until the penultimate page, and then no great hope is attached to their prospects. Marcuse's pessimism, like the optimism which preceded it and unlike the optimism which was to follow it—*One-Dimensional Man* was first published in 1964—is only very loosely supported by an appeal to evidence. He says that "the most telling evidence" for his view can be obtained by simply looking at television or listening to AM radio for one consecutive hour for a couple of days, and refers to a range of authors from Congressional committees to Vance Packard. But there is no attempt to use evidence in a rigorous way, and perhaps this is scarcely surprising, since in the 1960 preface to *Reason and Revolution* Marcuse wrote of what he called "the power of the given facts" that "this power is an oppressive power." But the given facts still have to be described correctly. Does Marcuse do this?

The fundamental thesis of *One-Dimensional Man* is that the technology of advanced industrial societies has enabled them to eliminate conflict by assimilating all those who in earlier forms of social order provided either voices or forces of dissent. Technology does this partly by creating affluence. Freedom from material want, which Marx and Marcuse himself took and take to be the precondition of other freedoms, has been transformed into an agency for producing servitude. When men's needs are satisfied, their reasons for dissent and protest are removed and they become the passive instruments of the dominating system. Marcuse is not insensitive to the apparently paradoxical character of the claim that in satisfying men's needs we may dominate them, and he tries to draw a distinction between false and true needs. False needs are "those which are superimposed upon the individual by particular social interests in his repression";[1] the difficulty with this definition is that it identifies false needs simply as those by which the individual is dominated, but it is clear what Marcuse means. Insofar as the individual's needs

[1] *One-Dimensional Man* (Boston, 1964), p. 5.

for material goods, for example, are gratified at the expense of his and others' needs for liberty and other such goods, the former are what Marcuse calls false. Marcuse holds that individuals are not necessarily themselves the arbiters of what they truly need. "In the last analysis, the question of what are true and false needs must be answered by the individuals themselves, but only in the last analysis; that is, if and when they are free to give their own answer." And so long as they live in a society like our own, they are not free. The question with which I began therefore becomes urgent: how has Marcuse acquired the right to say of others what their true needs are? How has he escaped the indoctrination which affects others? The point is not to charge Marcuse with personal arrogance, but to underline the inescapable elitist consequences of his viewpoint. Marx in the *Third Thesis on Feuerbach* remarked that the doctrine that men are molded by circumstances and need to be remolded by new circumstances divides men into two groups, those who mold and those who are molded. Once again Marcuse revives a pre-Marxist doctrine. Marcuse's elitism will reappear in his writings as an explicit doctrine; but it is already the implicit presupposition of *One-Dimensional Man*.

The forms of consumption in an affluent society have a twofold effect: they satisfy material needs which might otherwise lead to protest; and they foster identification with the established order. "If the worker and his boss enjoy the same television program and visit the same resort places, if the typist is as attractively made up as the daughter of her employer, if the Negro owns a Cadillac, if they all read the same newspaper, then this assimilation indicates not the disappearance of classes, but the extent to which the needs and satisfactions that serve the preservation of the Establishment are shared by the underlying population."[2] The conditioning of the population by these consumption patterns is reinforced by, rather than created by, the mass media.

Moreover, the conditions of work in an advanced industrial society tend to render the worker passive. The rhythm of production in a semi-automated factory, the nature of skilled work, the increase in the proportion of white-collar workers all destroy any consciousness of being in opposition to the work system. So, above all, do the institutions of the welfare state, which by means of an administered standard of living dominates the lives of the recipients of its benefits. This is once again because to increase consumption is fatally to weaken any impulses toward self-determination.

We may recall at this point Marcuse's insistence in his earlier writings on the coincidence of the conditions of freedom with those of happiness. But now Marcuse may seem to be saying that men no longer want to be free because the welfare state and the affluent society have made them happy. Has he therefore retracted his earlier view? Not at all, for although Marcuse does speak of individuals being "satisfied to the point of happiness with the goods and services handed down to them by the administration," he makes it clear that this happiness is not true happiness. The leisure of modern society is not free, because leisure "thrives in advanced industrial society, but it is unfree to the extent to which it is administered by business and politics."[3] More-

2 Ibid., p. 8.
3 Ibid., p. 49.

over, the permissiveness of modern society is also an instrument of domination. In previous social orders the sublimation of sexuality was repressive, and orthodox Freudian theory entails that any desublimation would be produced only by an end to or lessening of repression. In *Eros and Civilization*, Marcuse had argued for a revision of Freudianism, principally in the interests of the possibility of a culture not based on repression; but he now draws on the argument of that book in arguing that desublimation has already occurred in our society, but that the forms in which it occurs are as repressive as ever sublimation was. For the release of libido is so controlled that sexuality, as it were, saturates the surface of social life—in the motifs of so much advertising, for example—and satisfies men without restoring to them the proper enjoyment of their own sexuality.

This last theme is original to Marcuse; but it is worth noting that Marcuse shares much of the preceding argument with writers who from his point of view must appear as defenders of the *status quo*. He agrees, for example, with Raymond Aron in seeing all advanced industrial societies as fundamentally alike. This is particularly evident in Marcuse's discussion of the Soviet Union, where he identifies trends parallel to those he discusses in the West. In Marcuse's case this doctrine seems to depend upon a fairly crude technological determination. He makes little or no reference to the possibility of particular national traditions or cultures having an effect on social development. When he discusses the possibility of the Third World developing independent social and political forms, his pessimism derives from his belief that the underdeveloped countries will need to develop just that technology which is the source of the social order of domination in the advanced countries.

Likewise when Marcuse argues that conflict has been basically eliminated he repeats part of the case made by Daniel Bell in *The End of Ideology* and by S. M. Lipset in *Political Man*. Marcuse, like Bell and Lipset, takes it that the changes in consumption and in the structure of the labor force and the institutions of the welfare state have domesticated the working class and the labor movement and have so made the classical Marxist doctrine of class conflict inapplicable to modern society. Both Marcuse on one hand and Lipset and Bell on the other seem to envisage the ending, or at least radical modification, of the conflict between the labor movement and capital as spelling the ending of ideological conflict. Hence the end of ideology doctrine is implicitly and surprisingly accepted by Marcuse.

The chief difference between Marcuse and these writers lies in his view of the politics of advanced industrial society. Even on this point there are resemblances, for Marcuse begins from the same picture of pluralism and consensus that Aron, Bell, and Lipset use. "Advanced industrial society is indeed a system of countervailing powers. But these forces cancel each other out in a higher unification—in the common interest to defend and extend the established position, to combat the historical alternatives, to contain historical change." This common interest is reinforced by the ideological specter of the Enemy; both the West and Communism use the notion of external and internal threats to extend centralized forms of domination. It is a commonplace of orthodox political science that government in parliamentary democracy is exercised by competing elites; Marcuse would probably not dissent greatly from this analysis but would argue that such elites can exercise power only in the interests of this system of near-total control.

In his writings of 1934 Marcuse argued that liberalism had as its natural successor totalitarianism. In 1960 he took the prevailing social order of the advanced countries to embody just such a totalitarianism. He was thus prepared to characterize in the same terms Hitler's Germany and the United States of Kennedy, Johnson, and Nixon—or at the very least he was committed to hold that there were strong and growing tendencies in the United States which may be characterized in key respects as resembling Nazism. But the totalitarianism of the present is expressed not in political dictatorship but above all in the elimination of a culture which embodies ideals subversive of and alternative to the *status quo*. Art has, in Marcuse's view, lost its traditional functions: "It is good that almost everyone can now have the fine arts at his fingertips, by just turning a knob on his set, or by just stepping into his drugstore. In this diffusion, however, they become cogs in a culture-machine which remakes their content."[4] Marcuse sees this as a flattening out of culture, a liquidation of the two-dimensional into the one-dimensional. Hence the title of his book. It is not, however, only in artistic and literary works that this one-dimensional quality is found. Language itself is degraded, in advertising, in headline captions, in journalese, in abbreviations, above all in a style whose concreteness prevents reflective, critical thought about the realities referred to. So language joins libido, welfare, and work as an agency of totalitarian domination.

But is it all true? It is certainly the case that

[4] Ibid., p. 65.

One-Dimensional Man transformed Marcuse from an academic chiefly known as an interpreter of Hegel to an international figure invoked by some on the Left as their intellectual patron saint. It is clear that many students have taken Marcuse's portrayal of contemporary society with extreme seriousness. Therefore if it were to be held that Marcuse's account of contemporary society is almost entirely unfounded, the question would arise as to why he has then been so influential. Nonetheless I do believe that his account is largely false and that the concepts which it brings to the study of contemporary society are at once confused and confusing.

In assimilating Nazi Germany to such societies as those of North America and Britain today, Marcuse can only assist in obscuring the small but genuine threat from the neo-Fascist right that does exist in those societies. For the very use of the word "totalitarian" blurs essential differences in a way analogous to that in which the Communists' use of the term "social Fascist" to refer to Social Democrats in Germany in the late nineteen-twenties and early nineteen-thirties fatally— and the word "fatally" is not metaphorical—obscured the distinction between their differences with Social Democrats and their differences with Nazis. For Marcuse, liberal institutions are incipient totalitarian institutions; in fact liberal institutions and practices such as trade unions, universities, and freedom of speech have to be defended as a precondition of any rational social advance at all. I shall consider the practice of free speech when I come to examine Marcuse's doctrine of tolerance. But it is clear that Marcuse's whole doctrine of the welfare state rests on a misunderstanding of both the past history and present structure of liberal societies.

For the institutions of welfare not only could not have come into being without continuous struggle, especially by organized labor, but are maintained in being only by continuous pressure. The steady erosion of welfare institutions, the continuous re-creation of poverty is a part of the truth about modern industrial societies which Marcuse never mentions. Nor is it merely the amount of welfare and the quality of welfare that is in question. What the coming of the welfare state meant in Britain, for example, was a change in the conception of human rights and of social responsibility; the inroads on welfare at various points in Britain in the last ten years, and especially the quite new tolerance of larger amounts of unemployment by a Labour government, have been marked by an accompanying weakening of that conception. The notion that the ruling elites are now able to treat welfare as an instrument of social control is at very best a quarter-truth, and a very dangerous one insofar as it distracts from concern over welfare.

Permissiveness in sexual matters is also a more ambiguous matter than Marcuse supposes. It is not at all evident that such permissiveness has as much effect on actual sexual behavior and attitudes as some believe, let alone on anything else. To be very concerned about permissiveness is the mark of one section of the intelligentsia, a section which, because of its hold upon the mass media, is apt to overimpress us. Indeed, it is beyond controversy that we have no worth-while evidence at all about the impact of changes in attitude to sexuality on political and social attitudes. What Marcuse asserts about this might, of course, be true; but he certainly has no good reasons for asserting it.

The case against Marcuse's view of advanced industrial society, however, is not just a case against each of his separate contentions. There are strong grounds for objecting to his whole conception of such societies. In the first place, we may question the view which Marcuse shares with Aron and with so many others that advanced industrial societies are all fundamentally of a piece. Marcuse believes this only partly because of the belief which he inherits from his Marxist past that the ultimate causal-agency in such societies is their technology. It is also that he takes such societies to be internally homogeneous, so that the area within which independent social factors might have effects is radically diminished and increasingly so. Marcuse's vision is of a single systematic web of interconnections by means of which each part of society is dominated in the interests of the total system. He apparently sees such societies as among the most highly integrated in human history. But just this is what is most dubious.

It is clear that technological advance and investment in such advance are the mainspring of the continuous expansion which underpins the real if precarious stability of advanced industrial society. This expansion affects to some degree every sector of the social order. But the degrees to which different sectors are affected, the rates at which they expand, and the directions in which they expand are quite different. The result is not the highly integrated and well-coordinated system portrayed by Marcuse, but rather a situation in which there is less and less coordination between different sectors. Followers of Marcuse often claim, for example, that the higher educational system has the function of producing and processing those whom the economy needs. Nothing could be further from the truth. In every advanced industrial society higher education has been expanded and the job structure enlarged and changed; but the relation between the two has been weakened, not strengthened, for the two expansions have simply not stood in any determinate relationship.

The feeling of impotence that many have is not misplaced. They are impotent. But they are not impotent because they are dominated by a well-organized system of social control. It is lack of control which is at the heart of the social order, and central governments reflect this impotence as clearly as anything else. The ideology of planning, of the effectiveness of central power, has become dominant just at the point in history at which planning, except within very narrow limits, is bound to be ineffective. The most impressive political fact of our time is the accidental character of most of the policies which government is forced to embrace, an accidental character whose peculiar quality springs from the combination of the uncontrolled nature of the events with the insistence of those who govern, dominated as they are by the ideology of planning, that events are in fact directed by their deliberate and willed purposes.

The paradigmatic example of political accident is the Vietnam war. The myth of American imperialism in Vietnam is the product of a collaboration between the sternest critics of the war and its sternest supporters. In actual fact, American involvement in South Vietnam came about through a series of improvisations and *ad hoc* measures in which Presidents Kennedy and Johnson continually produced larger and larger unforeseen effects; they then identified themselves with what they had produced and ended by producing a war which has been destructive for every party engaged in it and from which no good can result. The sternest critics of the Vietnam war, however, see this inhuman result as the deliberate action of wicked men; its sternest defenders, such as Dean Rusk and Walt W. Rostow, insist too on providing rationalizations which are intended to convey a thread of purpose where none was. If Rusk and Rostow were right, their critics would be right too. But both work within frameworks which demand of social life that it have a coherence which in fact it no longer possesses.

Just because of the discontinuities and disharmonies of advanced industrial societies, factors other than technology may play an important causal role. Political traditions, cultural institutions, decisive actions *may* all occasionally have far greater effects than they could have in the better-integrated societies of the immediate past, and these may lead different advanced industrial societies to change in quite different directions. J. B. Bury argued that the length of Cleopatra's nose was a determining factor in creating the Roman Empire; we too live in a Cleopatra's-nose age, when relatively small causes may have relatively large effects.

Moreover, Marcuse is quite wrong in supposing that the will to change must be absent for the majority in advanced industrial societies. Far from its being the case that such societies generate only needs and wants that they can satisfy, such societies continually create wants that they cannot satisfy, and those who govern them make promises that they cannot keep, partly because the horizons of purpose continually change, and partly because of the lack of control of events by government. The whole process of mass education unites both these features and is thus potentially disruptive. The disillusionment which ensues can, of course, be either creative or destructive in its effects. What will determine which it is, I shall have to discuss at a later stage in the argument.

Marcuse's claims in *One-Dimensional Man* did, of course, go beyond claims about the social order. He claimed, too, that the philosophical thought of the present, especially the philosophy that is prevalent in Britain and the United States, is corrupted by its conformist and uncritical character. Since Marcuse's arguments for his own philosophy depend in large part on his attempted refutation of this philosophical alternative, his indictment deserves to be examined in a little detail.

One-Dimensional Man:

The Critique of Modern Philosophy

vii

Marcuse's indictment of recent philosophy falls into two parts, one philosophical and one sociological. The sociological claim is that recent philosophy has the function of rendering men incapable of a rational criticism of the social environment. He speaks of such philosophy as helping "to coordinate mental operations with those in the social reality" and says of the philosophy which he characterizes as "linguistic analysis" (Wittgenstein, Ryle, Austin) that it has an "intrinsically ideological character." But this claim need not be discussed independently of Marcuse's philosophical characterization. If it can be shown, as I intend to show, that this philosophy does not possess the characteristics which he ascribes to it and in virtue of which he further ascribes to it a conservative sociological function, then Marcuse's sociological indictment must also fail.

It is worth noticing, as a preliminary, some of the less central features of Marcuse's treatment of philosophy. One is his way of lumping together very different thinkers under a common label for purposes of either castigation or commendation. This he does not only in his treatment of recent philosophy but in his discussion of "classical philosophy," with which he contrasts it in order to condemn it. So Marcuse can ask, "Who is, in the classical conception, the subject that comprehends the ontological condition of truth and untruth?" and reply in a paragraph whose only explicit reference is to Plato's *Meno*. The argument of this paragraph is that "in the classical conception" truth is accessible only to the philosopher-statesman and not "to anyone who has to spend his life procuring the necessities of life," but that "if men no longer had to spend their lives in the realm of necessity, truth and a true human existence would be in a strict and real sense *universal*. Philosophy envisages the *equality* of man but, at the same time, it submits to the factual denial of equality."[1] If by "philosophy" Plato is meant—and the mention of the philosopher-statesman as well as the allusion to the *Meno* supports this—then Marcuse's statement is plainly false. Plato never envisaged the equality of men and he did not think that it was because most men had to spend their lives in procuring the necessities of life that they lacked access to truth; Plato believed that some men were genetically incapable of rising to the truth. It is difficult to resist the conclusion that Marcuse actually minimizes the ideological content of "classical philosophy" in order to draw the contrast with recent philosophy that his thesis requires.

There are three foci for Marcuse's discontent with

[1] *One-Dimensional Man* (Boston, 1964), p. 129.

recent philosophy: its uses of formal logic, its pre-occupation with language and above all with ordinary language, and its philosophy of science. Marcuse's treatment of logic develops an assertion made by Horkheimer and Adorno: "The general concept which discursive logic had developed has its foundation in the reality of domination."[2] Marcuse supposes that logic's neutrality in respect of content, the fact that logic identifies and classifies statements and arguments in virtue of their form, amounts in some sense to a distortion of reality. "This general quality (quantitative quality) is the precondition of law and order—in logic as well as in society—the price of universal control."[3] There was a point in human history in which logic as an instrument of control not only was, but had to be, introduced. "The idea of formal logic itself is a historical event in the development of the mental and physical instruments for universal control and calculability."[4]

Marcuse's treatment of logic thus rests upon two closely linked ideas, that there was a point in human history at which thought was subordinated to and organized by the laws of logic, and that we can contrast thought prior to such subordination and organization with thought subjected to this control. Both these ideas are mistaken.

Certainly there is a point in the history of thought at which formal logic was discovered as a discipline. But men syllogized before Aristotle, and they did so because they had no alternative if they were to think at

[2] Max Horkheimer and T. W. Adorno, *Dialektik der Aufklärung* (Amsterdam, 1947), p. 25.
[3] *One-Dimensional Man*, p. 136.
[4] Ibid., p. 137.

HERBERT MARCUSE | 86

all. What logic does is to articulate and to make explicit those rules which are in fact embodied in actual discourse and which, being so embodied, enable men both to construct valid arguments and to avoid the penalties of inconsistency. The construction of valid arguments and the distinction between valid and invalid arguments are important not merely for intellectual inquiry. The notion of validity is already presupposed by the use of all those words in ordinary language which function as logical connectives, not only "because," "therefore," "implies," "if . . . then . . .," and the other more or less explicitly logical words, but also "and," "or," "but," and the like. Someone who understands the meaning of "James did come home" and "John went to the cinema," but who does not understand that if it is true that either James did come home or John went to the cinema, and that James did not come home, then it is true that John went to the cinema, has not understood the meaning of "if . . . then . . . ," or of "either . . . or," or of "not." That is to say, our understanding of those words so basic to a vocabulary as "not" and "or" presupposes an understanding of and an ability to make use of certain logical laws.

Moreover, if this were not so we would be involved in certain difficulties fatal not merely to the possibility of argument and therefore of rationality, but also to that of speech itself. For the laws of logic are rules accord with which is necessary if consistency is to be preserved and contradiction to be avoided. Marcuse takes it to be some kind of special doctrine of formal logic that "contradictions are the fault of incorrect thinking." It is perhaps the case that we owe it to formal logicians that we are as well-informed as we are about the nature of and the penalties to be paid for contradiction. But if Aristotle had never founded the discipline and if he had had no successors, contradiction would still be what it is and the penalties for it would still be paid. What are these penalties? The first is that the man who asserts that something is the case and then immediately denies precisely what he has just asserted, and who also tells us that he has not changed his mind, has succeeded in asserting nothing at all. Assertion and denial cancel each other out, and such cancellation is always and necessarily the effect of asserting and denying that something is the case. But this is not all. A pupil of Duns Scotus demonstrated that—without, incidentally, making use of a formal calculus—and C. I. Lewis followed him in demonstrating that from a contradiction any statement whatsoever can be validly derived. It follows that to commit ourselves to asserting a contradiction is to commit ourselves to asserting anything whatsoever, to asserting everything whatsoever that it is possible to assert—and of course also to its denial. The man who asserts a contradiction thus succeeds in saying nothing and also in committing himself to everything; both are failures to assert anything determinate, to say that this is the case and *not* this other. We therefore depend upon our ability to utilize and to accord with the laws of logic in order to speak at all, and a large part of formal logic clarifies for us what we have been doing all along.

This entails the falsity of Marcuse's view of logic. For the distinction between thought which accords with and thought which does not accord with the laws of logic is obliterated. Thought which did not accord with the laws of logic would have no coherent speech to express itself in. There could not be or have been—and there therefore in fact never has been—such thought.

There could not, moreover, be any point in the history of thought at which thought was subordinated to, organized by, or made subject to the control of formal logic. The whole metaphor of control is thus out of place, for it depends for its cogency on just that contrast between thought as yet uninformed by the rules of logic and thought so informed which the preceding arguments show to be mistaken. Marcuse's own high-handed scorn about those whom he criticizes makes it not inapposite to remark that the arguments which I have been deploying are very elementary ones, familiar to every student with the barest knowledge of logic. The suspicion is thus engendered that not only Marcuse but also Adorno and Horkheimer actually do not know any logic, and it is certainly the case that, if they do know any, all three have taken some pains to conceal their knowledge of the subject which they are professedly criticizing.

This suspicion is slightly reinforced by Marcuse's references to the differences between ancient and modern logic. He appears not to know that the Stoics anticipated some of the most important parts of modern logic, as did the medieval logicians—I have given one example above—and that Aristotelian logic can be devised as part of a more extensive system.[5] Marcuse says that "the sterility of Aristotelian formal logic has often been noted. Philosophic thought developed alongside and even outside this logic." But such accusations have been characteristically made in periods when formal logic had degenerated or disappeared. When Hobbes or the Cartesians or Locke made such accusations, they were able to do so only because they were

[5] See Jan Lukasiewicz, *Aristotle's Syllogistic* (New York: 1957).

confronted by a threadbare tradition which invoked the name of Aristotle to justify what was often non-Aristotelian.

Marcuse's charge of sterility, however, is perhaps not directed at logicians who fail to achieve what logicians can and ought to achieve, but based on a misconception of what logic is and can achieve. Logic is not a set of rules for making discoveries; it is not a heuristic. For this there is a very good reason. While we may make use of certain inductively supported rules in a rough and ready way to guide our attempts to solve problems, there are in a crucial sense no rules for making discoveries. The most attentive reliance to the problem-solving guidance afforded by such heuristic as exists may leave a man completely baffled by a new problem; a brilliant hunch may guide to the discovery of a solution a man who has flouted such guidance completely. We cannot avoid relying on the laws of logic both in framing hypotheses and in making deductions from such hypotheses in order to test them; and we may well draw on particular discoveries by formal logicians in thinking up hypotheses; but logic is not imagination, and the framing of hypotheses is necessarily a work of the imagination.

Marcuse's notion of a logic which is not formal, of a dialectical logic is committed to opposition to estab-not mark the distinctions between form and content or those between discovery and formalization as I have done. But Marcuse could not, for the reasons I have already given, even frame the notion of such a logic without relying on the very logic he disowns. Moreover, to make logic a matter of content as well as of form is precisely to endanger the non-ideological character of logic. Marcuse believes that formal logic is the logic of the "given reality" or "established reality," whereas dialectical logic is committed to opposition to established reality. But just because to assert anything at all or to propound any argument is to involve the canons made explicit by formal logicians, logic is subject-neutral. It is at the service only of valid argument, and it is just this subject-neutral character of logic that enables us to use it in criticizing established modes of arguments and so transcending them. Certainly logic will not protect any man from adopting false premises for his arguments; but only logic will show him to what he has committed himself in adopting them. Marcuse's blindness to this aspect of logic is part of his failure to discriminate between those parts of intellectual inquiry which are more and those which are less exposed to ideological corruption by the social order. Had he tried to carry through such a discrimination, he might have noted that enmity to logic is necessarily irrationalist. Since it is the irrationalism of modern society which Marcuse wishes to unmesh and whose sources he wishes to identify, his failure to understand the role of logic in intellectual matters is a symptom of the failure of his whole inquiry.

Marcuse's criticism of "linguistic philosophy" is not unaffected by his misunderstandings of logic. He also makes his own task unnecessarily difficult (and yet of course much easier) by lumping together the in fact very different views of Wittgenstein, Ryle, and Austin. A consequence of these two features of his thought is that he does not notice how the kind of concern which perhaps does underlie his worries about logic was in fact formulated very clearly by Wittgenstein. The whole drive of Wittgenstein's concern in the *Philosophical Investigations* is directed to showing that the structure of a language is very different from that of a calculus. A calculus may be consistent or inconsistent, complete or incomplete; a language cannot be any of these things. It is *we* who are on occasion inconsistent, not the language, or language. It follows that the rules of a language and what it is to follow the rules of a language are quite different from the rules of a calculus and what it is to follow the rules of a calculus. When Wittgenstein tries to construct language games in which builders carry stones but communicate and speak of what they are doing in ways quite different from those in which we do, or when he imagines tribes with practices quite different from ours, the whole point is to discover what could be otherwise in our linguistic practices and the rules that govern them and what could not. This is how we uncover the relationship between the meaning which key expressions in language possess and the basic forms of human life. Those who fail to understand this relationship do so perhaps because they are in the grip of some theory which leads them to produce mystifying and unintelligible locutions. One such theory which Wittgenstein attacked in the *Blue Book* was precisely that which springs from thinking "of language as a symbolism used in an exact calculus." Nonetheless we may in fact help to discover what is wrong with such a theory by comparing the rules of language with those of a calculus with a view to identifying the difference between them. This is one key philosophical use of formal logic.

This is enough to make clear why Marcuse's attack on Wittgenstein for giving so much importance to ordinary language is misconceived. Wittgenstein never denied that we need to introduce technical terms and he would never have denied that this may be necessary in philosophy as well as in other inquiries. But what he is concerned with is that such terms should not result in obfuscation. Marcuse once again takes to be an ideological component of recent philosophy a concern which is in fact necessary for the criticism of all ideology. We begin with ordinary language because that is what we all speak and without it we cannot communicate. But Wittgenstein's interest in ordinary language is an interest in discriminating the genuinely indispensable features of language and therefore of social life from those imposed upon us by distorting theories. Marcuse charges Wittgenstein with simply accepting the *status quo* because he insists that "philosophy may in no way interfere with the actual use of language; it can in the end only describe it."[6] But what Wittgenstein is insisting is that when philosophers present us with such striking claims as "We can be certain of nothing" or "We can never know what someone else is feeling" or "We do not perceive material objects," they cannot invent uses of language which will exempt them from the requirements of intelligibility imposed by "the actual use of language." That use must be described precisely in order to understand how mystifying theories are partly mystifying because and insofar as they evade these requirements. This is in no way inconsistent with asserting, as Wittgenstein also did assert, that "a reform of ordinary language for particular purposes, an improvement in our terminology designed to prevent misunderstandings in practice, is perfectly possible."[7] Wittgenstein did not believe, that is, that philosophy is to be used as an instrument for changing

[6] Ludwig Wittgenstein, *Philosophical Investigations* (New York, 1953), section 124.
[7] Ibid., section 132.

language; philosophy's task is clarificatory. Once again it is clear that Marcuse's criticism of philosophy rests on his Young Hegelian inflation of the claims of philosophy. Marcuse tries to make the specific criticism of specific social orders and an understanding of the task of changing them all part of the content of philosophy. But in exaggerating philosophy's claims, he misses what philosophy can achieve. On this topic too he misunderstands and misrepresents Wittgenstein.

Marcuse, having ascribed to philosophy the whole of intellectual inquiry—"to comprehend the world in which [individuals] live"—and thus having blurred all the important distinctions between the methods and uses of different types of inquiry, attacks the notion that philosophical analysis is essentially therapeutic. Now Wittgenstein did occasionally use therapeutic metaphors. But he saw philosophy's effect as being not so much that of *healing* as that of *liberating* us from false theories. It is extremely important that according to Wittgenstein philosophy is "not a theory, but an activity," that its tasks cannot be performed for one by others. The view of philosophical analysis as therapeutic in a sense analogous to that in which psychoanalysis is therapeutic was developed by John Wisdom rather than by Wittgenstein, and it is misleading so to characterize Wittgenstein's philosophical practice. For to become aware of what language and social life must be and therefore concomitantly of what is contingent and alterable is not something that can be completed in a once-and-for-all way, as a therapy can.

If what Marcuse says of Wittgenstein massively misses the point of Wittgenstein's work, the same is true of his attack on Austin. Austin's insistence that we attend to the common stock of distinctions embodied in ordinary language is an insistence that we protect ourselves from false and oversimplifying theories. So in his paper "A Plea for Excuses," Austin contrasts the multiplicity of distinctions that words such as "deliberately," "involuntarily," "inadvertently," "accidentally," and the like enable us to draw with the simple dichotomies too often relied on by philosophers in writing about responsibility. Marcuse says, "What is this 'common stock'? Does it include Plato's 'idea,' Aristotle's 'essence,' Hegel's *Geist*, Marx's *Verdinglichung* in whatever adequate translation?" But the point is that "idea," "essence," "*Geist*," and "*Verdinglichung*" embody theories, and theories which stand in reach of rational criticism. To criticize them we have to find a standpoint with as minimal a theoretical commitment as possible; this the study of the distinction embodied in ordinary language goes some way toward providing, even if it is, as Austin himself emphasized, a point of departure and not at all something that dictates our final conclusions. Austin in this study follows Aristotle closely, and his discussions of responsibility are clearly rooted in that in the *Nicomachean Ethics*. Hence Marcuse's attempt to exhibit a fundamental contrast between Austin's work and classical philosophy is misconceived.

Marcuse is at pains to emphasize the philosophical dangers involved in discussing the meaning of sentences in abstraction rather than the meaning given to sentences by actual speakers uttering them on particular occasions, and he clearly believes that in this emphasis he is in opposition to work such as Austin's. But it is in fact to Austin that we owe the first systematic attempt to understand the relationship between the meaning of sentences and the force of speech-acts. A systematic classification of types of utterance is a precondition of understanding how the meaning of sentences may be related to their use in social contexts. Once again it is just those to whom Marcuse ought to have learned to be indebted that he attacks.

Marcuse's attack on recent preoccupations with logic and with language is accompanied by an attack on the positivistic attitude of much contemporary philosophy of science. Marcuse takes modern science to be linked not merely empirically but conceptually to modern technology. "The principles of modern science were *a priori* structured in such a way that they could serve as conceptual instruments for a universe of self-propelling, productive control; theoretical operationalism came to correspond to practical operationalism." Such a passage makes it clear too that when Marcuse attacks operationalism—and he in effect identifies positivism with operationalism—in the philosophy of science, he is not attacking it because it gives us an unfaithful account of science. The whole project of modern science is seen by Marcuse in such passages as essentially linked to forms of domination. Marcuse stresses that his view is not incompatible with drawing a distinction between pure and applied science. Pure science is oriented to technology because it is neutral in respect of any particular use to which it may be put, because it has the form of an instrument. Is Marcuse right in this, and if he is, is he correct in connecting the fact with operationalism?

Operationalism is a doctrine in the philosophy of science formulated by P. W. Bridgman, according to which we are to understand a scientific expression in terms of the operations we perform in testing statements which contain it. "In general," wrote Bridgman, "we mean by any concept nothing more than a set of operations: the concept is synonymous with the corresponding set of operations."[8] It was independently formulated, but is closely related to, the verification principle formulated by members of the Vienna Circle, according to which the meaning of a statement is the method of its verification. Objections both to operationalism and to verificationism have been framed which are far more cogent than any suggested by Marcuse; but such objections are disregarded by him, perhaps because his fundamental objection to positivism is such that it could hold against any philosophy of science, especially if it has implications for the philosophy of meaning.

The reason for this is that Marcuse wishes to insist that the meaning of the key terms in philosophy—and they are the key terms of his own argument—is to be understood as giving them a more than empirical reference, and not in the way in which the theoretical concepts of science have a more than empirical reference. Speaking of universals such as "beauty," "freedom," and "whiteness," Marcuse asserts that "the substantive universal intends qualities which surpass all particular experience, but persist in the mind, not as a figment of imagination nor as mere logical possibilities but as the 'stuff' of which our world consists." This is to revive a long-standing Marcusean doctrine, which appeared in the essays of the thirties as the doctrine of essences. Marcuse is right to see a threat to this doctrine in the contemporary philosophy of meaning. For in order to persuade us that sentences such as that which I have just quoted are not hopelessly confused, he would have to produce an account of the meaning of his

[8] Percy W. Bridgman, *The Logic of Modern Physics* (New York, 1927), p. 5.

Marcuse's Program

VIII

At the end of *One-Dimensional Man* Marcuse saw only one chance of revolutionary protest, and that was "nothing but a chance." The chance was that "the substratum of the outcasts and outsiders, the exploited and persecuted of other races and other colors, the unemployed and unemployable" might turn to radical action. This would involve a meeting of "the most advanced consciousness of humanity and its most exploited force." But the critical theory of society can give us no grounds for predicting that this will happen; indeed it is of the essence of critical theory that it cannot predict. So Marcuse in 1964.

In 1969, in *An Essay on Liberation*, which professes to develop further the ideas of *Eros and Civilization* and of *One-Dimensional Man*, the whole perspective has changed. Utopia is actually at hand, its possibilities inherent in the technology of the advanced societies. What, then, prevents its presence? Not just forms of political organization. The rational reorganization of society and the establishment of genuine collective control by the working class would not abolish domination. We cannot take as our political maxim "To each according to his needs," because what stands in the way of Utopia is precisely the needs which men possess at the moment. These needs must undergo a "qualitative change" if men are to be liberated. Marcuse now aspires to provide a biological basis for his theory. His biology is in fact as speculative as his metaphysics, and Marcuse explicitly disavows any scientific basis for his speculations. This does not, however, lead him to be less than dogmatic in his mode of assertion. "Once a specific morality is firmly established as a norm of social behavior, it is not only introjected—it also operates as a norm of 'organic' behavior; the organism receives and reacts to certain stimuli and 'ignores' and repels others in accord with the introjected morality, which is thus promoting or impeding the function of the organism as a living cell in the respective society."

This view is used as the basis for a political theory in which the implied elitism of *One-Dimensional Man* is made fully explicit. Human nature is indefinitely malleable. The human nature of those who inhabit advanced industrial societies has been molded so that their very wants, needs, and aspirations have become conformist—except for a minority, which includes Marcuse. The majority cannot voice their true needs, for they cannot perceive or feel them. The minority must therefore voice their needs for these, and this active minority must rescue the necessarily passive majority.

This passive majority includes the working class, even the new, technically skilled working class. "This 'new working class,' by virtue of its position, could disrupt, reorganize, and redirect the mode and relationships of production. However, they have neither the interest nor the vital need to do so: they are well integrated and well rewarded."[1] Who are the minority who are to rescue the majority by transforming them?

Marcuse's collection of revolutionary forces is a list so familiar in fashionable radical circles that we must be careful not to miss its extreme heterogeneity: the student movement in the United States, the black population of the urban slums in the United States, the Chinese cultural revolution, the National Liberation Front in Vietnam, Cuba. There are three elements in this collection: there are first the genuinely aspiring poor of America and peasants in Vietnam and elsewhere, who must not be confused with their self-appointed spokesmen; there are the middle-class whites of the SDS and their counterparts in Britain, Germany, and France, who in their combination of insurrectionism and anarchism exemplify what Lenin diagnosed as left-wing Communism, an infantile disease; and there are the representatives of the Communist bureaucracies in China, Cuba, and Vietnam, who represent right-wing Communism, an oligarchical disease. These forces have only one thing in common: they are in conflict with the governments of the advanced industrial societies. But, as both Marx and Lenin knew, to be in conflict with the established order is not necessarily to be an agent of liberation.

Marcuse devotes most of his account of the forces of liberation to an argument about the character of the

[1] *An Essay on Liberation* (Boston, 1969), p. 55.

student revolts; what leads him to take them to be authentic agents of liberation is above all their aesthetic quality, their style. Flower power, the language of the hippie subculture, that of soul culture, the use of four-letter words mark, so Marcuse claims, a new sensibility which breaks with the culture of the market. What traditional Marxism saw as petty-bourgeois bohemia closely allied to the *Lumpenproletariat* has become in Marcuse's latest theoretical stance the potential catalyst of change. Traditional Marxism took the view that it did for a very good reason: that the sensibility of bohemia effectively cuts it off from the vast mass of mankind, on whom the bohemians are in economic fact parasitic. So, of course, are Marcuse's idealized students, who have produced the first parent-financed revolts in what is more like a new version of the children's crusade than a revolutionary movement. But this isolation in values of bohemia is just what Marcuse values, and the problem of communication with, of joint action with the majority does not arise, because the majority are to be objects of benevolent revolutionary concern, not subjects with an autonomous voice of their own.

In his essay on "Repressive Tolerance"[2] Marcuse argues that the tolerance of the advanced industrial democracies is a deceit. The expression of minority views is allowed just because it cannot be effective; indeed the only types of expression it can have render it ineffective. The major premise of his whole argument is once again that the majority are effectively controlled by the system and so molded that they cannot hear or understand radical criticism. It follows that the people

[2] In *A Critique of Pure Tolerance*, written with R. P. Wolff and Barrington Moore, Jr. (Boston, 1967).

have no voice and the alternatives are not between genuine democracy and the rule of an elite, but between rival elites, the repressive elite of the present and the liberating elite of the Marcusean future. Freedom of speech is not an overriding good, for to allow freedom of speech in the present society is to assist in the propagation of error, and "the telos of tolerance is truth." The truth is carried by the revolutionary minorities and their intellectual spokesmen, such as Marcuse, and the majority have to be liberated by being re-educated into the truth by this minority, who are entitled to suppress rival and harmful opinions. This is perhaps the most dangerous of all Marcuse's doctrines, for not only is what he asserts false, but his is a doctrine which if it were widely held would be an effective barrier to any rational progress and liberation.

The oddest feature of Marcuse's theory is perhaps that he has taken over from liberal and right-wing critics of the European revolutionary tradition a theory which they falsely ascribed to the Left, but which was rarely held until Marcuse espoused it. Both the Jacobins and Lenin believed in a temporary dictatorship of the majority over counterrevolutionary minorities—whatever they may have practiced. But it was left to Marcuse to profess a belief in a dictatorship by a minority.

What, then, are the true connections between tolerance, rationality, and liberation? The telos of tolerance is not truth but rationality. Certainly we value rationality because it is by rational methods that we discover truth; but a man may be rational who holds many false beliefs, and a man may have true beliefs and yet be irrational. What is crucial is that the former has the possibility of progressing toward truth, while the second not only has no grounds for asserting what he believes, even though it is true, but is continually liable to acquire false beliefs. What is it to be rational? It is a necessary condition of rationality that a man shall formulate his beliefs in such a way that it is clear what evidence would be evidence *against* them and that he shall lay himself open to criticism and refutation in the light of any possible extreme. But to foreclose on tolerance is precisely to cut oneself off from such criticism and refutation. It is to gravely endanger one's own rationality by not admitting one's own fallibility.

One of the most urgent of contemporary tasks is to insist on subjecting the social and political order to continuous rational criticism and to preserve the autonomy of rational inquiry in universities and elsewhere. The institutionalization of rationality was one of the great achievements of bourgeois society. Of course the very fact of institutionalization can be used to try to isolate the practice of rational criticism and so prevent it from being exercised upon the social order; and there is a continuous pressure upon universities and other institutions to make the practice of rational inquiry merely instrumental to the purposes of government. These assaults upon rational inquiry in the interests of the established social order have to be resisted. The new Marcusean radical case against tolerance makes those radicals who espouse it allies in this respect of the very forces which they claim to attack, and this is a matter not just of their theory but also of their practice. The defense of the authority of the university to teach and to research as it will is in more danger immediately from Marcuse's student allies than from any other quarter—even although Marcuse himself has on occasion exempted the university from his critique.

My view that tolerance and rationality are intimately connected is not merely an *a priori* thesis. The transformation of Marxism from a rationally held into an irrationally held body of theory is a transformation which was the result of Marxists cutting themselves off from possibilities of criticism and refutation. The use of state power to defend Marxism as the one set of true beliefs in the Soviet Union produced the atrophy of Marxism and the irrationality of Soviet Marxism. Not only was this use of state power repressive in respect of tolerance; it was the instrument of a minority who took up toward the majority an attitude very similar to that which Marcuse advises his minority elite to take up to the majority. The majority was in the Soviet Union the passive object of re-education in the interests of its own liberation. What Marcuse invites us to repeat is part of the experience of Stalinism.

One cannot liberate people from above; one cannot re-educate them at this fundamental level. As the young Marx saw, men must liberate themselves. The only education that liberates is self-education. To make men objects of liberation by others is to assist in making them passive instruments; it is to cast them for the role of inert matter to be molded into forms chosen by the elite. The majority of men in advanced industrial societies are often confused, unhappy, and conscious of their lack of power; they are often also hopeful, critical, and able to grasp immediate possibilities of happiness and freedom. Marcuse underrates most men as they are; the false contempt for the majority into which his theory leads him underpins policies that would in fact produce just that passivity and that irrationalism with which he charges contemporary society. The philosophy of the Young Hegelians, fragments of Marxism, and revised chunks of Freud's metapsychology—out of these materials Marcuse has produced a theory that, like so many of its predecessors, invokes the great names of freedom and reason while betraying their substance at every important point.

SHORT BIBLIOGRAPHY

INDEX

SHORT BIBLIOGRAPHY

I have listed here only Marcuse's major works. A full bibliography is available in *The Critical Spirit: Essays in Honor of Herbert Marcuse* (Boston: Beacon Press, 1967), edited by Barrington Moore, Jr., and Kurt Wolff.

A Critique of Pure Tolerance (with R. P. Wolff and Barrington Moore, Jr.). Boston: Beacon Press, 1967.

Eros and Civilization. Boston: Beacon Press, 1955.

An Essay on Liberation. Boston: Beacon Press, 1969.

Negations. Boston: Beacon Press, 1968. Although recently published, it contains the major essays from the nineteen-thirties.

One-Dimensional Man. Boston: Beacon Press, 1964.

Reason and Revolution. New York: Oxford University Press, 1941; reissued with additional material, New York: Humanities Press, 1955. Quotations in this book are from the later edition issued as a paperback, Boston: Beacon Press, 1960.

Soviet Marxism. New York: Columbia University Press, 1958.

INDEX